PORTLAND

BEER

CRAFTING THE ROAD TO BEERVANA

PETE DUNLOP

FOREWORD BY ANGELO DE IESO

AMERICAN PALATE

Published by American Palate
A Division of The History Press
Charleston, SC 29403
www.historypress.net

Copyright © 2013 by Pete Dunlop
All rights reserved

Front cover photo by Brent Bradley, Oregon Scenics. Back cover photography by Pete
Dunlop.

First published 2013

Manufactured in the United States

ISBN 978.1.60949.881.8

Library of Congress CIP data applied for.

For the founding craft brewers and their assorted allies.

CONTENTS

FOREWORD

It's hard to explain the culture of craft beer in Portland to someone who has never experienced it. With a rich history dating back to the nineteenth century, when Henry Saxer and Henry Weinhard begat German artisan brewing influence to the Willamette Valley, beer has always played an important role in the lives of Portlanders. Over the past 160 years or more, beer's significance here has, as it has in many regions, withstood many obstacles—Prohibition, world wars, economic depression and recession. None of these events has been able to knock the wind from the sails of enthusiasts' pursuit of their chosen malted beverage. In fact, it appears that these trials have served mostly to ignite an even more powerful enchantment for great beer.

While other regions and cities have deeply ingrained histories of beer making, the proliferation of dynamic styles that we are witnessing in Portland is astounding. Looking around this unique area, one might question why good beer carries so much significance here. Is it the extraordinarily soft water available from the Bull Run watershed? Is it the abundance of regionally available hops that thrive in the Willamette Valley and the Yakima Valley to the north? Is there something culturally instilled in the collective identity in the Rose City? Inquiring minds want to know.

Since the 1860s, Portland has maintained a bustling pub culture that still manifests itself today. Some credit our passion for a rich tipple to the gray and gloomy months filled with seemingly never-ending precipitation. Whatever it is, the change in seasons provides a suitable canvas for involving ourselves in a vast and ongoing spectrum of beer styles, even those that are conducive to the hot, dry summers that many outsiders don't realize we experience each year. When it comes to beer, anyone who is honest understands Portland's well-deserved position at the forefront of all things related to the culture of the product. Portland is home to more breweries within its city limits than any other settlement in the world. Data gathered by the Oregon Brewers Guild shows that the state of Oregon ranks in the nation's top three in number of breweries, breweries per capita, craft beer production, craft beer consumption and percentage of draft beer consumed.

And it's not just raw statistics like brewery count that bolster our city as the best; it is also the passion and interest that follow suit. Look around at just about any pub in Portland. From dive bar to diner pub, virtually all of Portland's watering holes offer at least a few craft beer options for those who pursue more than a multinational, adjunct-riddled industrial lager.

Today, breweries in Portland are unabashedly knocking down conventional barriers and carving out discerning niches in flavor and style. The possibilities seem endless, and the future seems blindingly bright. Craft beer is a fixture in Portland, whereas in other regions it represents a smaller segment of those inevitably lured by more esoteric tastes. Here, beer appears to be a part of our genetic code. It is a binding cultural component of our collective identity, as well as an important pillar of our economy. Our city's need to embrace progressive, artistic and forward-thinking ideals shows itself in our propensity to choose locally sourced, sustainable, good-tasting products. Do we drink more great beer because it is available, or do we produce more great beer because it is what we elect to consume? These pages will discuss and answer some of these questions. Of course, you are cordially invited to experience Portland firsthand and formulate answers of your own.

Cheers!

ANGELO DE IESO
Founder, Brewpublic.com

Photo by Damian DeBuiser.

PREFACE

I am a firm believer in the people. If given the truth, they can be depended upon to meet any national crisis. The great point is to bring them the real facts...and beer.
—Abraham Lincoln

The idea for this book first occurred to me several years ago, while we were in the midst of a significant expansion in the number of craft brewers here in Portland. There were about forty-five breweries at the time, if memory serves, more than any city in the world. I figured it would be worthwhile to investigate how and why craft beer became such a big deal here. Of course, few of us knew what was to come. New breweries continued to open. Today, there are more than fifty operating breweries in Portland, with a dozen more on the fringe of the city. And there are more on the way. There are many worthy beer histories from cities with great craft beer cultures and a surplus of breweries, but Portland's is one that must be told.

For the record, I first became aware of craft beer in the mid-1980s, while I was a graduate student at Washington State University. There were very few craft breweries in those days and none anywhere near Pullman. But one or two of the better watering holes had jumped on the craft beer bandwagon. A tennis buddy of mine had been playing tournaments around the Northwest and apparently discovered craft beers on his travels. One day, after playing a few sets, we visited a local watering hole, and he introduced me to Hale's Ale. I didn't love it, but I instantly realized that it was different than anything I had experienced growing up in rural eastern Washington.

Preface

Like the rest of my generation, I grew up in an era dominated by light lagers. My dad had permissive attitudes when it came to beer, so I grew up tasting lots of beers. There wasn't much to taste in industrial lagers that relied on the color of the can and advertising slogans to attract fans. Coors was the gold standard for us, and it was available across the river from my boyhood hometown of Clarkston, Washington. Many preferred Coors for its premium identity…or Miller for the clear bottle…or Budweiser for the red, white and blue labeling. Northwest beers Olympia, Rainier and Lucky Lager were cheap and readily available, and people often settled for them in place of the national brands. People argued a lot over which beers were the best. But the differences were nearly nil. These were the virtual dark ages of beer.

I was mostly oblivious to the shift that was beginning to occur about the time I sipped that first Hale's Ale. My own drinking tastes from the mid-'80s on centered on Henry Weinhard's Blue Boar and the occasional import. The first microbrew I tasted in a bottle was Bert Grant's Scottish Ale. He founded his brewery in Yakima in 1982, and at least one store in Pullman carried Grant's beers, which were on the hoppy side for their day. Indeed, Grant himself was apparently known to carry a vial of hop oil on his travels so he could bring pedestrian macro beers to life. Grant, who passed away in 2001, is possibly the father of the heavily hopped, aromatic IPA style that is so popular in the Northwest and around the country today.

When I arrived in Portland in early 1989, the craft brewing industry was still in its early stages of development. McMenamins, Widmer Brothers Brewing, Portland Brewing and Bridgeport Brewing were all established and humming along. The McMenamins model was the plainest to see because by the early 1990s, it was everywhere. McMenamins was crucial to the early development of the craft beer industry in Portland because there was almost always one nearby when you found yourself in the mood for a decent beer. Portland Brewing, Widmer and Bridgeport weren't quite as accessible, but they were growing as well. The craft beer industry was small compared to what it is today, but it was established and gaining momentum.

The quintessential questions include: How did it happen here? What was it about this city that fostered its runaway brewery count? Is it because the water here is exceptional and easy to come by? Is it because quality hops and grains are grown in the fields not so far from Portland? Does it have something to do with the city's strong brewing and pub culture dating back to the nineteenth century? Is there something about the weather here that gets citizens fired up to flee their homes and spend afternoons and evenings quaffing beer in comfortable pubs? Are the undercurrents of local

Portland beer fans don't mind standing in line for great craft beer. *Courtesy of Timothy Horn and the Oregon Brewers Festival.*

ingredients and production so strong that people are driven, increasingly, to artisan beers and foods? Those are among the topics for consideration in the following pages. Stick around.

WORDS OF WISDOM

This book is primarily a work of nonfiction about breweries, pubs and beer. I have to assume anyone reading along is interested in visiting these places and sampling the beers. Please partake in moderation. If you have to drive where you're going, a designated driver is a good thing. If you're walking or riding a bike, use the same sort of cautions. Be advised that Portland has a viable public transit system, including bike taxis, and there are great tours to help beer fans explore the city's beer culture.

ACKNOWLEDGEMENTS

Although there were a few people who never quite bought into this project, there were many more who did and helped make it happen. The fact that I've lived in what is arguably the center of the craft beer universe in Portland for nearly twenty-five years gave me a head start in some sense. The people I met and experiences I had likely could not have happened anywhere else. Some of the people who lent me assistance are local, and some are from my recent and not-so-recent past. The common theme is that they contributed in some significant way to what you will read in these pages. It goes without saying that these folks bear no responsibility for errors in judgment, fact, grammar or structure.

The book certainly could not have happened without the help of Art Larrance, a founding brewer who remains active via the Oregon Brewers Festival and Cascade Brewing. When I was interviewing Art for another project in 2011, we discussed the idea of a book on Portland's brewing history. Art supported the idea from that moment on and repeatedly offered to help in any way possible. He never wavered from that commitment, connecting me with key people and giving me access to his own collection of documents and memorabilia. Art introduced me to Bryan Anderson, who gave me unlimited access to his *Alt Heidelberg* collection of beer artifacts dating to the nineteenth century, as well as his own knowledge of the pre-Prohibition era. Jeff Alworth, who has been writing thoughtfully about Portland's beer culture and beer generally for many years, offered helpful suggestions and connected me with key sources. Finally, there is no book without a publisher.

ACKNOWLEDGEMENTS

The folks at The History Press wanted this book and allowed me to write it. Thanks to Aubrey Koenig and everyone there for their assistance.

Special thanks are due Angelo De Ieso (aka Brewpublic) for writing a foreword that provides his view of Portland beer. Angelo is a generation behind me, and I hope his contribution will persuade young beer fans to learn more about Portland's rich beer history. Many people provided valuable input and insight via interviews, correspondence, photos and other materials and suggestions: Kurt and Rob Widmer, John Harris, Fred Bowman, Karl Ockert, Dick and Nancy Ponzi, John Foyston, Lisa Morrison, James Fick, Tom Mason, Brian McMenamin, Jerry Fechter, Gary Fish, Chris Crabb and Donna McCoy. Special photo credits are due Jane Zwinger, Mark Zusman (*Willamette Week*), Matt Wiater (portlandbeer.org), Jay Brooks (brookstonbeerbulletin.com), John Klatt (Old Oregon Photos) and Mary Hansen (City of Portland Archives). I'm quite sure I've left some people out, and to those folks I apologize.

I have to recognize some folks from my days at Washington State University. Gene Clanton guided much of my undergraduate and graduate work and remains a friend. The late Edward Bennett directed my master's degree program and steered me in the direction of better writing. John Jameson, whom I worked for as a research and teaching assistant, was a significant influence. I owe much to the folks I worked with on the *Daily Evergreen* staff from 1986 to 1988—people like Kathleen (Gilligan) Coleman, Dan Nelson, John Hill, Joe Hudon, Lois Breedlove and Don Ferrell. I've had some pretty amazing professional colleagues, as well, but none more important than Bill Langenes. I worked alongside Bill in corporate marketing communications for seven years. Coincidentally, the job offer he extended when I went to work with him was signed at Alameda Brewhouse in Northeast Portland. Go figure.

Family and friends have been important, too. My dad, the late John Dunlop, introduced me to beer at a young age and was a homebrewer long before it became fashionable. His beers (and wines) were dreadful, but at least I saw what he was trying to do—probably more so later when I started brewing myself. We later enjoyed many fun times at the Oregon Brewers Festival. Lyle Raffety, my stepdad, doesn't necessarily share my taste in beer but has always enjoyed tipping one back and talking about it. From my days in Pullman, Doug Flansburg is a friend who first introduced me to craft beer one day after playing tennis. After my arrival in Portland, my now longtime friend Tony Maiorca continually pushed me to explore the craft beer scene during the early 1990s. I attended the Oregon Brewers Festival with Tony for the first time in 1991, truly a revelation. There are countless others.

Finally, you can never give enough credit to those whose support is vital to turning an idea into something tangible. My wife, Laura, put up with me through the gradual genesis of this project. I'm sure she thought the idea was quite insane, but she went along with it. Family members and friends also supported the idea and were happy to offer constructive (and not so constructive) suggestions. Everyone was happy to drink great beer while talking about the project. In the not-to-be-overlooked department, I couldn't have done one iota of this without the gracious companionship of my Labrador dogs, Blitz (nope, not named for the beer) and Biscuit. Biscuit slept on the pad next to my desk while I wrote most of this; Blitz checked in occasionally but mostly slept on the couch upstairs. They have difficult lives, these two.

A good many beers were obviously sacrificed during the course of completing this project. Inquiring minds may wonder which one was my favorite. I have to borrow and slightly modify the words of the immortal Fred Eckhardt in that regard: "My favorite beer is very often the one in my hand...or my next free one."

Cheers!

PROLOGUE

I am sure Americans can fix nothing without a drink.
—*Frederick Marryat in* A Diary of America

From the viewpoint of modern Portland, to say nothing of the craft beer boom that is happening around the country, it's easy to get carried away when you think about the importance of beer in America. Many modern imbibers simply assume beer has always been the nation's beverage of choice. That myth has been perpetuated by stories of the Pilgrims coming ashore in New England because they had run out of beer. Then there's the one about the Founding Fathers brewing their own beer. It's quite an elaborate picture. However, these stories mostly serve to confuse the issue of what Americans were drinking for much of our early history, at least until the 1850s.

English and Dutch settlers were engaged in small-scale commercial brewing by the mid-seventeenth century. The climate and terrain around present-day New York were well suited to growing barley and hops, thus facilitating brewing. There were twenty-six breweries and taverns in New Amsterdam by 1660. It was common for colonial households to brew their own beer. We know George Washington made beer for his family and servants, as well as possibly for himself. Commercial brewing remained small scale and local until after the Civil War due to the fact that beer did not travel well. That situation improved in the second half of the nineteenth century, thanks to advancements in packaging and transportation. The reality is that other alcoholic beverages were more popular than beer until that time.

Hard cider was popular, made from apples and other fruits crushed and fermented on homesteads across the land. Making cider was possible anywhere fruit could be grown and did not require fancy equipment or expertise. However, distilled liquor was the beverage of choice in early America. Rum and whiskey were the rage. By 1763, rum was being produced by 159 commercial distilleries in New England alone. Liquor was so plentiful by 1820 that it was cheaper than tea. By 1830, there were 14,000 distilleries in the United States, and American adults were consuming seven gallons of pure alcohol per capita every year. That's the equivalent of 1.7 bottles of 80-proof liquor per person, per week—roughly 90 bottles a year for every American adult, including those who didn't drink.

The shocking rate of alcohol consumption created enough societal dysfunction that it eventually led to the initial temperance movement. Americans looked in the mirror and didn't like the reflection. A serious crusade began in the 1820s. But enforced limits on alcohol sales and consumption often led to discontent and rioting in cities where it was tried. Americans soon saw consumption as a personal issue. Millions pledged to abstain from or moderate their alcohol consumption between 1820 and 1850, and it was working. By 1840, annual per capita alcohol consumption had fallen to just three gallons. Temperance became synonymous with moderation rather than all-out prohibition. It was through this door that beer stepped to become the alcoholic beverage of choice in the second half of the nineteenth century.

But before beer could truly step to the forefront, it needed to change. The only beer known to early Americans was English-style ale. There are plenty of good reasons why it was never as popular as cider or spirits. First, you needed equipment, ingredients, basic brewing know-how and reasonable sanitation to create something drinkable. Those things were in short supply. English-style ale brewed in early America often had the taste and texture of muddy water. It was sometimes sweet, sometimes sour and consistently inconsistent. It also didn't stay drinkable for very long once tapped, typically turning sour. Those who could afford it preferred bottles imported from proficient brewers in Great Britain. Many could not afford that option. Thus, homemade cider and distilled spirits were wildly popular.

All of this was turned upside down with the arrival of a new generation of European immigrants during the 1840s. Many came from Germany and brought recipes for a different kind of beer and the means to produce it. Of the 4.3 million immigrants who came to the United States during the 1840s and 1850s, some 75 percent were of Irish and German descent. The Irish were mostly poor peasants fleeing the famine that ravaged their primary food source and devastated their island. The Germans were different. They were more likely to be educated and of middle-class means. They came to America to escape the political and economic gridlock of their homeland, where royal tyrants crushed dissent and thwarted ambitions. Unlike the Irish, many Germans arrived with a bit of money and a craft with which they could make more. They filtered out to all corners of the country, and some of them built breweries where they produced lager beer.

Lager turned the fortunes of American beer around. We aren't talking about the fizzy industrial lager that rose to great popularity in the twentieth century. Lager produced by nineteenth-century brewers was generally darker and more substantial than what came later. "Lager," from the German verb *lagern*, means to store or rest. The beer is fermented at lower temperatures with slower-acting yeast than ale. Many of the artifacts that cause off-flavors in ale end up as harmless sediment in lager. More than that, lager held up better than ales and usually didn't turn sour. Lager was mostly impossible in the United States before the mid-nineteenth century for two reasons: first, the yeast cultures were fragile and didn't travel well across the ocean until faster clipper ships were in common use; second, the cold storage needed to make lager was problematic in most places prior to the advent of industrial refrigeration. (Early lager producers relied on ice cut from frozen lakes and streams in the winter to create makeshift fermentation and storage facilities.) Once established, lager caught on because it was clean, consistent and offered a low-alcohol alternative to cider and spirits. It fit in perfectly with the mood of the country at just the right time.

Lager is much more than the beer that made Milwaukee famous. It also helped launch droves of new breweries in cities and towns across the young United States. One of these places was Portland, which experienced a significant influx of new residents during the 1840s and 1850s. Many of the immigrants were important, but one's name would become synonymous with beer for more than one hundred years.

CHAPTER 1

BEGINNINGS

WEINHARD'S BEACHHEAD

It took my eye. I had no idea of laying out a town there, but when I saw this, I said: "Very well, sir, I will take it."
—*land speculator Asa Lovejoy's recollection of his first view of the land that would become Portland, while in the company of William Overton*

Settlement of the Oregon Country was underway by the 1820s. What was initially a trickle became more than that in the 1840s, when thousands came to the Willamette Valley seeking free land and the chance for a better life. The discovery of the Oregon Trail and an 1846 agreement that set the formerly disputed border between the United States and British North America at the forty-ninth parallel helped spur an increase in migration. The bulk of those who came to Oregon came to settle the land or work at logging, fishing or similar vocations. This wasn't the case in California, which was the preferred destination of fortune hunters who often had no plans to stay. But the discovery of gold in California in 1848 had a significant impact on the development of Portland and Oregon.

In the days before the railroads came to the Northwest, trade moved up and down the Columbia and Willamette Rivers. The land that became Portland was claimed in 1843 when Asa Lovejoy paid twenty-five cents to record a joint claim (with William Overton) to a one-square-mile claim on the west side of the Willamette River a few miles downstream from Oregon City. Overton, who saw the area's potential but had no funds, soon sold his half-interest to Francis Pettygrove, an Oregon City merchant. The name of the fledgling city was determined in 1845 when the two partners flipped a coin. Pettygrove won the flip, and his choice of Portland, after the main seaport in his native Maine, won out over Lovejoy's choice of Boston. Lovejoy soon sold his interest to Benjamin Stark, who effectively exited the partnership with Pettygrove in 1847, leaving the latter in control of the new city.

The outset of the California Gold Rush in 1848 nearly wiped Portland out. Many able-bodied men fled the city (really just a frontier village) to seek their fortunes to the south. By one account, only three men remained in Portland at the end of the year. Believing his business prospects to be poor, Pettygrove liquidated his assets and high-tailed it to California. Before leaving, he sold the entire townsite claim to Daniel Lownsdale, more or less forsaking his partnership with Stark. Although the gold rush initially damaged Portland's well-being, it soon became a catalyst for dramatic growth. The key element was the city's geographic location next to deep water with ample space for docks. Portland soon nipped the ambitions of Oregon City, Milwaukie and other nearby towns as the center of Oregon's trade with California. Lumber was the key exported item initially. Even the poorest-quality lumber could easily be sold at an enormous profit, and Portland took the lead in the Northwest lumber industry once a steam-powered sawmill went into production in 1950. An average of five ships per month came in and out of Portland in early 1849. The monthly average had jumped considerably by the early 1850s.

Portland was nothing more than a village at the time. The city, nicknamed "Stumptown" due to the presence of abundant fir stumps, sported a population of just 821 in 1850. The stumps, remnants of numerous felled fir trees, were scattered generously throughout what constituted the center of town, whitewashed to reduce the possibility of nighttime collisions. Although small, Portland was the largest city in the Northwest and would be so for many years. The fledgling city was of greater strategic and economic importance than Seattle until the 1880s, when the coming of the railroads facilitated the movement of goods from inland areas to the more substantial seaport in Puget Sound. But all that is somewhat inconsequential to our story, which is concerned with beer and brewing in Portland.

Commercial brewing in Oregon got underway with the arrival of German-born Henry Saxer in 1852. Saxer arrived via Illinois and opened the first brewery in the Oregon Territory, which then included present-day Oregon, Idaho and Washington. His Liberty Brewery was located at what is now First Avenue and Davis Street. Much has been made of the possibility that Saxer set up shop in Portland because he recognized the quality of the water and the Northwest's potential for growing hops and grain. That seems

Portland was a frontier outpost in 1852, as shown in this view of Front Avenue looking south from Alder Street. *Courtesy of Portland City Archives.*

rather quaint in retrospect. What he likely saw was a small town packed with a growing number of seamen, longshoremen, lumbermen, fishermen and related laborers who were or would be thirsty for beer. The population of Portland was largely made up of men under the age of thirty, and the saloon boom was just beginning by 1851. Saxer almost certainly knew a good business opportunity when he saw one.

Saxer wasn't alone. Other breweries soon followed in towns around the Northwest. Beer was entirely a local affair in the frontier Northwest. There was simply no way to efficiently transport bulky kegs, really the only beer packaging at the time, any distance. Thus, frontier towns invariably had their own small breweries to supply the local workforce. Saxer's brewery happened to be the first in the Northwest. Within a few years, the original structure had grown to include several two-story buildings. Portland experienced rapid population and economic growth through the 1850s, and business was good. For reasons apparently related to his health, Saxer sold his brewery to Henry Weinhard in 1862 and returned to his native Germany. The Weinhard name would become synonymous with Oregon beer for more than a century.

Weinhard was born in 1830 in Lindenbronn, Wurtemberg, Germany. He attended school there and entered a brewer's apprenticeship in Stuttgart. Weinhard was a fast learner and by age twenty-two was looking for an opportunity

The iconic founding father of Portland brewing was Henry Weinhard. *Library of Congress photo.*

to make his mark in the world as a brewmaster. As mentioned earlier, Germany was in a state of political and economic disarray by the late 1840s. The country was undergoing a transformation from a mostly agrarian society to a more industrialized one. The political system was controlled by elites and royalty, with most citizens locked out. Young Germans who wanted to maintain their status looked for a place where land and opportunity were plentiful. It was with that in mind that the United States became the destination for many. South America and Mexico were also popular destinations.

With visions of prosperity on his mind, Weinhard crossed the Atlantic in 1852. He soon made his way to Cincinnati (some accounts say St. Louis), where he worked in a brewery or breweries for several years. Hearing stories about high demand and little competition in the Northwest, he traveled to Philadelphia and boarded a ship bound for Oregon via the overland Isthmus of Panama. Weinhard landed at Fort Vancouver in the Washington Territory in the spring of 1856. Founded by the Hudson's Bay Company in 1824–25 on the north bank of the Columbia River, Fort Vancouver was the economic and social hub of the Northwest for the next twenty years. It acted as the center of the fur trade and helped attract new settlers to the area.

New to the area and uncertain as to where to find the best opportunities, Weinhard went to work for Muench's Vancouver Brewery, recently established by John Muench and located very near Fort Vancouver and its captive clientele of eight hundred thirsty soldiers and laborers. After six months in Vancouver, Weinhard migrated to Portland and entered into a partnership with George Bottler, who was operating a small brewery on present-day Couch Street and Front Avenue. Why Weinhard moved is not entirely clear. It appears that Civil War tensions caused a portion of the troops garrisoned at Fort Vancouver to ship out, which meant a shrinking beer market. Also, Weinhard likely saw that Portland was on its way to becoming the center of commerce in the region and would soon outstrip Vancouver in both population and prospects. Portland in 1856 had a population of roughly 1,200 but would have nearly 2,900 by 1860. The future Rose City was experiencing a dramatic growth spurt at a time when the fortunes of the Hudson's Bay Company and Fort Vancouver were in decline. The move to Portland made sense.

But the arrangement with Bottler did not work out. Growth and profits were not what Weinhard had hoped for. Although he maintained ties with Bottler, he packed his things and returned to Vancouver in early 1857, again going to work in John Muench's brewery. Two years later, he purchased the Vancouver Brewery. There he brewed his beer and bided his time while plotting the right moment to return to Portland. On its face, the retreat to Vancouver seems to make little sense. Portland was growing rapidly, while the area around Fort Vancouver was in disarray and decline. The move makes the most sense if viewed as part of a larger effort to build capital and plan something bold for Portland.

Several years later, in 1862, Weinhard returned to Portland and purchased Henry Saxer's Liberty Brewery. He appears to have held onto the Vancouver operation until 1864, when he sold out to Anton Young. The purchase of Saxer's brewery was a quintessential moment in Oregon brewing history. Weinhard quickly acquired a larger piece of property away from the downtown core and soon relocated the brewery, which was renamed the City Brewery. Recurrent spring floods of the downtown area almost certainly helped prompt the move. The site on West Burnside is where Weinhard Brewing and later Blitz-Weinhard resided until 1999. A portion of the old brewery is today occupied by Henry's Tavern. It's interesting to note here that the founding of Weinhard Brewing is typically listed as 1856. That seems a bit of a stretch. Weinhard may have arrived in the Northwest in 1856, but he wasn't established in Portland until 1862.

The City Brewery was a big success, benefiting from the city's rapidly growing population. Portland offered a larger market and ready access to many business opportunities. It's worth noting that Portland and the Northwest were largely untouched by the Civil War, except to the extent that supplies and building materials were needed to fuel the war and postwar effort. Weinhard soon expanded his operation to meet growing demand for his beer with additional structures, including a house near the brewery where he lived with his wife, Louise, and their children. By 1870, Portland's population had surpassed 8,000, and the City Brewery was producing two thousand barrels of beer annually. Before the craft revolution of the 1980s,

Spring floods like this one (from 1876) were common in Portland and may have convinced Henry Weinhard to build his new brewery on higher ground. *Courtesy of John Klatt and Old Oregon Photos.*

the period between 1870 and 1900 was arguably the golden age of brewing in Portland. The population skyrocketed from about 8,300 in 1870 to more than 46,000 in 1890. It passed 90,000 by 1900. The wild growth fueled opportunities in many areas. A number of new breweries opened to serve the burgeoning population, although most of these breweries lasted only a few years. Weinhard continued to consolidate and build his empire in a number of ways, not all of them specifically related to beer.

Thinking about the extent to which beer became the dominant alcoholic beverage in Portland, it's important to consider the demographics of the population. During the second half of the nineteenth century, Portland attracted a huge number of young men who came to work in the extraction economy (the labor-intensive process of harvesting Oregon products and putting them on ships for export). There were plenty of folks who came to farm and ranch in rural areas. But the men who came to the city lived and worked there. Beer was the beverage of choice because it was the most readily available. City workers weren't in a position to manufacture hard cider or spirits. They worked long, hard hours processing logs, loading and unloading ships or performing general labor. At the end of the long workday, workers wanted a beer. And it was available. This was a shared experience in many frontier towns and cities.

A flock of new breweries opened in hopes of capturing a share of the burgeoning market between 1870 and 1890, with more to come after 1890. Some had more success than others, but none challenged the supremacy of Weinhard's City Brewery. The short-lived breweries included Belinger-Weiss Brewery (1879–84), South Portland Brewery (1882–85), Jubitz and Scheland Brewery (1874–76), Schaefer & Burelbach Brewing (1886–87) and Britannia Brewing (1887). It was fairly typical in those days for breweries to open and be sold or closed within a few years. This happened with successful and less successful operations. The longer-lasting, more successful breweries included the following.

East Portland Brewing, founded by Henry Ludwig in 1870, was located at Union Avenue (now Martin Luther King Boulevard) and Washington Street in what was then East Portland. The area on the east side of the Willamette River was annexed to Portland in 1891. Ludwig sold beer in bottles and kegs for several years. He sold the brewery in 1878, and it was closed in 1884.

The Gambrinus Brewery was established in 1875 by Louis Feurer. This was a large operation that consumed several blocks in the area of Twenty-second Avenue and Flanders. Gambrinus enjoyed a good reputation, and Feurer had sold nearly 1,100 barrels of lager in 1879. The facility moved to a new location on Washington Street in 1892. After twenty years in business, Feurer sold the plant in 1895, and it continued to operate until state prohibition came in 1916. The Gambrinus plant was reopened under a new name in the 1930s, and the name itself has significance in modern times. In fact, one might argue that Gambrinus is still brewing in Portland. But these are all details to be covered later.

United States Brewing joined the mix in 1873, located on Front Avenue between Clay and Columbia Streets. George Herrall, from Baden, Germany, was the brewer. The place was initially known as the Eagle Brewery, but

If happy thou
wouldst be,
And healthy
all the year,
GAMBRINUS
LAGER BEER
Let be
"THE BEER"
for thee.

Gambrinus Brewing was opened in 1875 and closed at the outset of state prohibition in 1916. This table display is from 1915. *Courtesy of Bryan Anderson.*

switched to US Brewing in 1876. Herrall sold 1,506 barrels of lager in 1878 and moved the operation to East Portland the following year. There he built a four-story brewing plant and residence. US Brewing did well, and Herrall eventually sold beer in California and Canada. The brewery closed when he died in 1896.

Against the background of a growing population and increased competition, Weinhard's City Brewery flourished. He sold two thousand barrels of lager in 1870, and his output increased steadily thanks to distribution beyond the local community. By 1882, City Brewery was the largest in the Northwest and still growing rapidly. Weinhard, a student of manufacturing efficiency and excellence, realized it was time to upgrade his facilities and create a modernized "monument to brewing." The existing wood structures on West Burnside were replaced by an entire block of brick with an immense brewhouse at its core. To comply with federal law, which mandated that bottling facilities be separate from brewing operations, Weinhard located his bottling plant across Couch Street. Nearby, he built stables for the horses that pulled beer delivery wagons. On the waterfront, he had a warehouse in which to store beer in transit. The enterprise was renamed Henry Weinhard Brewery.

Weinhard was always focused on producing a quality product and getting it into the hands of consumers in a timely fashion. However, delivering beer to saloons and other customers could be challenging in late nineteenth-century Portland. Unimproved streets were often made muddy and impassable by rainfall and floods. Beer wagons were often stuck in the muck and unable to move. In 1889, the *Oregonian* labeled Portland "the filthiest city in the northern states" due to its horrendous network of sewers and

Portland's streets were often muddy or flooded during the fall, winter and spring. It was only mildly muddy the day this photo was taken next to the Weinhard Brewery in 1905. *Courtesy of John Klatt and Old Oregon Photos.*

gutters. Another publication described sidewalks then recently installed as "a disgrace to a Russian village." Henry Weinhard's response to the transportation challenge was to boast in ads, "My beer can be shipped to any portion of the globe, to any climate and [is] warranted not to sour." He began shipping his flagship Columbia Lager throughout the West during this period, and he also shipped beer to Asia. You have to wonder if challenges related to navigating Portland's often impassable streets prompted Weinhard to look for outside markets.

As historian Herman Ronnenberg has suggested, successful brewers of the period almost always diversified their holdings to include other properties and businesses. Weinhard was an entrepreneur as much as he was a brewer, and he expanded his holdings considerably during these years. He financed or helped finance the construction of numerous buildings in the downtown area. In 1890, he built the Grand Central Hotel on Third Street. The hotel was a model of modern technology of the day, with steam heat, electric lights and fine furnishings. Like other city leaders of the day, Weinhard also invested in businesses. He owned or partly owned several saloons,

SKIDMORE FOUNTAIN BEER CAPER

Stephen Skidmore was a longtime Portland resident who arrived with his parents at age twelve in 1850 and served as one of the first carriers of the newly founded Oregonian newspaper. He later established a successful drug business and served on the city council from 1875 to 1878. Upon his death in 1883, Skidmore bequeathed $5,000 for the building of a large fountain that would provide drinking water for people, horses and dogs.

The city council appointed a committee to manage the fountain project. Lawyer Charles Wood, who had connections with artists outside Portland, was put in charge of selecting an artist to design it. Wood selected a friend, Olin Warner, who was then considered one of America's elite sculptors. The envisioned fountain wound up costing $18,000 instead of $5,000. Skidmore's business partner and longtime friend, Charles Sitton, and friends Henry Failing and Tyler Woodward donated the additional funds necessary to construct the fountain.

When it was completed, Wood was considering how to unveil it when Henry Weinhard suggested the idea of running a hose from his brewery and pouring free beer from the fountain. City leaders considered the idea but eventually declined. There has been speculation that the city feared that its valued fire hoses (it was nearly three-quarters of a mile to the brewery) would be torn apart by thirsty Portlanders or that they wanted to avoid a drunken frenzy (people and horses) at the unveiling. Good possibilities. Another idea is that this was a snub. Despite his wealth, German immigrant and brewer Weinhard was never quite accepted by the city's teetotaling elite.

Skidmore Fountain as it appears in modern Portland, still exactly where it was originally located. *Photo by the author.*

Today, Skidmore Fountain is still much as it always has been. Although modern Portlanders may not appreciate it, the fountain is designed just as Skidmore requested. It has three tiers: a lower one for dogs, a middle one for horses and an upper one for people. The fountain was placed in what was then a busy thoroughfare as a sort of centerpiece of the community. Shortly after it was completed, the business district shifted to the southwest. City leaders have considered moving the fountain on several occasions, but it hasn't happened.

including one attached to his brewery. People often point to Portland's strong pub culture as being part of what fostered the interest in good beer over time. Quite possibly. But the saloons of the late nineteenth century would eventually lead to trouble.

In addition to being a brewer and entrepreneur, Weinhard was regarded as something of a philanthropist. He evidently gave generously to a variety of charities and supported municipal and public projects. When a Portland bank failed, he informed its president that he would have provided the funds necessary to keep the institution afloat had he known of its plight. It was likely a combination of his business and civic-minded interests that drew him into the legendary Skidmore Fountain story.

Stephen Skidmore, a Portland druggist, passed away in 1883. In his will, he set aside $5,000 for the construction of a large drinking fountain in the center of the downtown business district. In charge of the project was writer, painter and attorney Charles Wood, who also happened to be Henry Weinhard's attorney. With construction complete, Wood was considering the plan for unveiling it when he met with Weinhard. The brewer suggested connecting the fountain to his largest tank of lager with a long hose (it was a fair distance to the brewery) and thus share free beer with the local citizenry via the fountain. This idea was considered by city leaders and eventually turned down, but the story is legendary and a great example of Weinhard's civic generosity and business sense.

While Weinhard was busy building his beer business and other enterprises, national brands began appearing around the Northwest. There were several things driving this. First, the discovery of pasteurization allowed bottled beer to be stored and shipped long distances without spoiling. Before this time, beer in bottles typically turned sour after a short period. Second, the transcontinental railroad was linked to Portland and much of the Northwest.

Anheuser-Busch beer was present in Oregon well before this 1908 photo. *Library of Congress photo.*

Sealing bottles remained something of a problem for brewers and wouldn't be fully solved until the invention of the modern crown cap in 1892. In the interim, most bottles used cumbersome wired corks, similar to what we see on specialty beers and champagne bottles today.

Adolphus Busch was one of the first to recognize the business potential presented by the combination of pasteurization and the national railroad network. Anheuser-Busch quickly implemented pasteurization and began shipping its beer to California, Oregon and the rest of the country. This was effectively the beginning of national brands, and it was used by Weinhard and other regional brewers to expand their markets on a smaller scale. Anheuser-Busch eventually leveraged a refined national strategy to squash competition and dominate the American beer market. This changing reality also brought labeled packaging so beers could be easily identified. That had never been an issue when most beer was served on draft, but the growth of bottled beer changed all that.

Henry Weinhard barely noticed the impact of national brands. His output reached forty thousand barrels in 1890. He continued to dominate the Portland market by supplying beer to a network of commercial outlets and saloons, some of which he owned or had an interest in. As if following the lead of Anheuser-Busch, he took advantage of new business realities by selling his beer to customers up and down the Pacific Coast and in the inland Northwest. Beer from Weinhard's brewery also found its way to international markets in China, Japan, the Philippines and, oddly enough, Siberia. These were great times for the Weinhard Brewing Company. Employees earned good wages and had great job security. There were rumblings of trouble in the form of the temperance movement, which would inflict serious harm on the brewing industry in Oregon and around the country. But things were good for now.

CHAPTER 2

WRONG WAY

ROAD TO PROHIBITION

The stench of stale beer and whisky often mixed with the nauseating smell of vomit on the sidewalks, and drunken staggering men blocking my way almost turned my stomach.
—schoolteacher Lucy Adams commenting on Portland's saloons upon her arrival in 1902

Portland was rapidly turning into something more than a dank frontier community by the 1890s. The population nearly doubled from 46,000 to 90,000 during the decade and would more than double to 207,000 by 1910. This was the last triple-digit population increase by decade in the city's history. Just as important, demographics were changing. A city that was once made up primarily of young laboring men was transitioning to one with families and kids. This evolution would come to present a number of challenges for city leaders as early as the 1880s, as they grappled to address the needs and desires of a changing community. On the cusp of coming upheaval in the world of beer and alcohol, Weinhard Brewing continued its growth and additional breweries opened. Serious issues were dead ahead as the mood of the city, state and country changed.

Henry Weinhard Brewing cruised through the 1890s, selling 100,000 barrels of lager annually by 1900. The brewing machine on West Burnside had been built with production efficiency and capacity in mind and was succeeding. The company's flagship beer, Columbia lager, was popular throughout the West and had a following in foreign markets. To fully

This view of Portland from 1894 shows a growing city with numerous landmarks. The castle-like structure near the middle of the frame is the Portland high school. *Courtesy of Portland City Archives.*

consolidate his position in the Northwest, Weinhard bought out competitors in Eugene and Roseburg and installed ice production facilities. The ice was used to supply Weinhard storage facilities in those cities and others. Cold storage was crucial to the beer manufacturing and storage in those days. Before the development of ice-making equipment, ice was cut from lakes and rivers and awkwardly carted to breweries and storage warehouses. The advent of ice-making machines, which were initially the size of a building, changed the game. Having available cold storage in communities outside the Portland area helped Weinhard extend his reach.

Additional breweries continued to pop up in Portland even as the steady march toward state prohibition gained momentum. This would be the last expansion of the brewing trade in Oregon before the craft revolution of the 1980s. Most of these businesses didn't survive long, although one of them turned out to be quite significant.

Wilhelm Brewery, located in the Sellwood area and also known as the Sellwood Brewery, opened its doors in 1893 and was operated by John Wilhelm until his death in 1902. His widow, Mary, kept the place open until

The building that housed Arnold Blitz's Portland Brewing Company still stands tall on Northwest Upshur. *Photo by the author.*

1904. As was often the case, the Wilhelm Brewery had an attached saloon and an affiliated saloon in the downtown area.

Portland Weissbeer Brewing and Bottling operated in Milwaukie from 1902 to 1907. The brewery specialized in Weissbeer, a light, Bavarian-style beer usually brewed with wheat and minimal hops. Weissbeer is the virtual polar opposite of the hoppy IPAs that became popular in Portland (and around the country) a hundred years later, but the style has made a comeback with some contemporary beer fans. Mt. Hood Brewing, a name that would pop up again later, operated on East Water Street from 1905 to 1913. North Pacific Brewing was operated by John Kopp from 1905 to 1911. This was the Portland branch of Kopp's main facility in Astoria. Enterprise Brewing also operated during this time.

The most significant operation of this period, outside Weinhard Brewing, was the Portland Brewing Company. Arnold Blitz, a former Studebaker executive, bought a half interest and later a controlling interest in Portland Brewing after he arrived in 1904. The brewery operated at Northwest 1991 Upshur until state prohibition came in 1916. As with other breweries, Blitz produced syrups and nonalcoholic drinks to survive. His name would become synonymous with Oregon when Portland Brewing merged with Henry Weinhard Brewing to form Blitz-Weinhard in 1928.

Throughout the second half of the nineteenth and early twentieth centuries, the brewing industry and its connected businesses were dogged by the temperance movement. As mentioned earlier, the roots of that movement date to the 1820s, when the country was awash in hard liquor and consuming it readily. Some part of the anti-alcohol sentiment was pacified by the growing popularity of lager beer starting around 1850. Then the Civil War intervened to thwart the efforts of prohibitionists. This was at the national level. Oregon toyed with prohibition in the 1840s when the territorial legislature passed a law outlawing the production or sale of spirits in 1844. The law didn't address beer and was repealed a year later. It reemerged several years later, in 1854, when a women's group petitioned the territorial legislature to ban liquor. The petition was denied.

Oregon was the first of the Northwest states, admitted to

Edel Brau was the best known of the beers produced by Arnold Blitz's Portland Brewing Company prior to prohibition. *Courtesy of Bryan Anderson.*

the union in 1859 largely due to the strategic and economic importance of the Columbia River. The temperance movement in Portland was always on the prowl, and it gained increasing traction over time. The principal reason was the saloon culture. A little perspective may be in order. The number of saloons in the United States ballooned from 100,000 to 300,000 between 1870 and 1900. Portland, in 1893, had 245 saloons. While the temperance movement made much of the evil role of alcohol in the saloons, beer and other booze were not the most serious social concern. These places were havens of gambling and prostitution. Husbands and fathers would slink into saloons after work and fail to come home. Or they would come home penniless and drunk as skunks.

Arguably the most infamous of Portland saloons was Erickson's, established in the 1880s by Augustus Erickson. Patrons could drink, gamble, play billiards, get their shoes shined, socialize or sample one of the establishment's many hostesses. Erickson's was a city within a city. It was considered the finest saloon in town by workingmen and consumed a full block on Burnside between Second and Third Avenues. The bar wrapped around the interior and was 684 feet long. Patrons were treated to a hearty free lunch at Erickson's for the price of a five-cent beer. The saloon was such an important part of the culture that during the great flood of 1894, Erickson rented a houseboat and filled it with booze, food and other necessities. Customers in rowboats, canoes and makeshift rafts paddled to the houseboat to get what they needed. Erickson's is just one example of the strong saloon culture that existed in Portland in the pre-Prohibition era. While they may well have formed the basis of the city's longstanding pub culture, saloons were considered dens of ill repute by the temperance movement, whose mission was to shut them down.

Revenue and corruption issues aside, the clearest and most serious obstacle to temperance and prohibition in the late nineteenth century was women's suffrage…or, more precisely, the lack thereof. From the beginning, the movement to do something about the alcohol problem was led predominantly by women. It's not so hard to understand why. Women were the ones who most often found themselves victimized by the specter of gambling, prostitution and habitual drunkenness. Yet they were powerless to do anything about it because they had no direct political standing. Even as Portland became a more gender-neutral city in the 1890s, women could do little to address a political and economic system that sheltered the saloon culture.

Women were, nonetheless, highly involved in movements that pushed for temperance. In 1874, the newly formed Portland Temperance

TEMPERANCE AND TAXES

One of the more serious obstacles faced by temperance advocates was financial and involved both federal and local government. The federal government had implemented an excise tax on alcohol to help finance the Civil War. The brewing industry initially opposed the tax and got it reduced from one dollar to sixty cents a barrel after the war. Still, the tax accounted for one-third of federal revenues by 1875. Almost by osmosis, the industry realized that it wasn't such a bad thing for the government to be dependent on them for revenue. The tax gradually increased in ensuing years to the point that temperance forces described it as "a bribe on the public conscience." The government's dependency on revenue from alcohol taxes was a serious obstacle to national Prohibition until the federal income tax was established in 1913.

Portland's situation was similar to and in some ways worse than what was happening at the federal level. By 1880, the city was getting one-third of its annual revenue from liquor taxes. There was no way to tax illegal gambling or prostitution, common features of the roaring saloon culture. But you could tax liquor, and that's what the city did. This reality effectively blocked the temperance movement. It also caused city leaders and police to look the other way when it came to enforcing existing ordinances against vice and prostitution. This matter was made worse by the fact that many of Portland's wealthiest and most eminent citizens owned or had interests in the saloons and related businesses that needed policing. Henry Weinhard was one of them. It became clear to temperance leaders that vice and prostitution were moneymaking propositions quietly sanctioned by the city's most prominent business leaders.

A federal tax stamp from 1878. Beer taxes helped keep the government afloat during and after the Civil War and postponed national Prohibition. *Courtesy of Art Larrance.*

Crusade, initially composed of twelve activist women, descended on a popular downtown saloon known as the Webfoot. This led to month-long confrontations between seemingly fearless women and saloon supporters. After the women were arrested for disturbing the peace, a judge dismissed the charges. The women returned to the scene and were arrested again. This led to a court case and a guilty verdict for six women. When the convicted women refused to pay the imposed five-dollar fine, they were sentenced to twenty-four hours in jail. However, the police chief refused to put them in jail, and they were released. The women did not win their battle to shut down the Webfoot, but the incident underlined the seriousness of their movement and helped attract new crusaders to the ranks.

One of the most important proponents of temperance was Abigail Duniway, who arrived in Portland with her family in 1871. Duniway soon befriended local minister Thomas Lamb Eliot, already a vocal opponent of Portland's saloon culture, which he described as the "black hole of Calcutta." Eliot and Duniway soon found themselves working toward similar goals in alternate ways. Where Eliot tended to be reasonable and soft-spoken, Duniway thrived on personal attacks. She charged Portland's city government with "notorious laxity" in enforcing anti-prostitution laws and claimed that it enforced laws against "wandering cows" more strictly. In fact, Duniway never truly believed in the temperance movement. She understood early on that the only way to address the saloon problem was through the ballot, and she used the temperance movement to draw women into the push for suffrage. As we shall soon see, women's suffrage wound up being the key to state prohibition in Oregon.

CHAPTER 3

PROHIBITION

AN UNWANTED DISASTER

Why don't they pass a constitutional amendment prohibiting anybody from learning anything? If it works as well as Prohibition did, in five years Americans would be the smartest race of people on Earth.

—Will Rogers

Oregon reached its pre-Prohibition peak of forty-eight breweries around 1890. These were predominantly small breweries, with a single brewmaster, that produced just enough beer to serve local customers. Weinhard Brewing was an obvious exception, as was North Pacific Brewing in Astoria. The brewing industry's move toward efficiency, consolidation and extended markets was in full swing by the 1890s. Weinhard's ambition and vision may not have matched that of Adolphus Busch, but he was following a similar path. His acquisition of breweries in the region solidified the dominant position of Weinhard Brewing in Portland and around the Northwest. The strategy also helped the company survive the Prohibition years and positioned it to flourish when repeal came.

Prohibition did not come to Oregon in sledgehammer fashion. Instead, it came in a series of steps that led to local and eventually state prohibition. With the tax issue removed via establishment of the federal income tax, the move toward national Prohibition gathered steam and was eventually implemented. The brewing and saloon industry was losing the battle in the early years of the century. Things would get a lot worse before they got better.

It was fairly obvious from earlier attempts to realize prohibition that Oregonians as a whole had no stomach for it. National groups began to get involved in the battle by the 1880s with little success. When the national Prohibition Party and the Women's Christian Temperance Union (founded in 1874) managed to get a prohibition measure on the Oregon ballot in 1887, it was defeated by a three-to-one margin. That was the last prohibition measure to be placed on the state ballot for seventeen years, but the movement remained active in other ways. Through a series of strategizing meetings, the national groups eventually became convinced that brewing and liquor interests controlled the legislature and could buy the outcome of state elections. Thus, they attacked the issue from the angle of local control.

Local choice in the matter of saloons had been provided for since before statehood. Anyone wanting to open a saloon in a community was required to submit a petition containing signatures of citizens who lived in the precinct equal to a simple majority of the total vote in the last election. The law proved effective in keeping saloons out of small communities, but it had little impact in larger communities like Portland. Cities had the power to license saloons but not to prohibit them. Dry forces knew full well, based on

Temperance certificates like this one were signed and carried by temperance advocates as proof of their commitment to the cause. *Courtesy of Art Larrance.*

the behavior of Portland's local government, that saloons and their affiliated illicit businesses were unevenly regulated. The idea behind local control was to remove alcohol from city council politics. The opening they needed came in the form of initiative and referendum, adopted by Oregon in 1902.

Once in place, the initiative and referendum process allowed prohibitionists to get the local option bill on the ballot in June 1904. With help from the Anti-Saloon League (founded in 1893) and Women's Christian Temperance Union, the local option bill passed by a vote of 43,316 to 40,198. Dry forces now turned their attention to the fall election and getting the local option passed in counties across the state. In the end, twenty-six counties voted on county prohibition; it passed in six, mostly by meek numbers. It did not pass in Multnomah County, where it was not supposed to have appeared on the ballot in the first place. During the campaign, the measure received a thorough whipping in the *Oregonian*, which said it would retard business growth. Weinhard Brewing unsuccessfully attempted to have the measure removed from the ballot and then invested in getting it defeated.

The local option led to a convoluted, checkerboard situation in which wet and dry counties were neighbors. You couldn't buy beer in one county, but you could buy it in the one next door. Then came home rule laws that further complicated the mess by allowing cities within the same county to enact their own prohibition laws. Lane County was dry, and you couldn't buy alcohol in Eugene. But Springfield, also in Lane County, was wet. Many Eugene residents made regular trips to Springfield, basically a small lumber community at the time, to purchase booze.

None of the prohibitionist victories had any significant effect in Portland or Multnomah County. As has been documented in numerous places, the prohibition movement was made up largely of religious figures and elitist women's groups. Their message resonated much more strongly in rural America than it ever did in cities. This was true in Oregon, as well. In Portland, the Anti-Saloon League and WCTU had little credibility or standing. When the league held a meeting in early 1905, coverage in the *Oregonian* suggested the group lacked interest in its own cause. When an Anti-Saloon League man was stabbed in Salem in early 1906, the *Oregonian* gleefully reported the sordid details. Although the competing *Oregon Journal* sided with drys, the idea of prohibition was not well received in the Rose City.

State prohibition likely never would have happened in Oregon had it not been for one rather crucial development. In November 1912, the men of Oregon voted 61,265 to 57,104 to give women the vote. This was not a novel idea, particularly in western states where there weren't a lot of

The city's vibrant saloon culture was on display at Groh's Saloon in this 1903 photo. *Courtesy of Portland City Archives.*

women. Giving them the vote was a way to make women feel better about living in or coming to Oregon. There was also a stronger sense of shared responsibility in areas that had once been part of the frontier. That surely swayed the votes of many men. Once women had the vote, Oregon was targeted by prohibitionists. There were already a number of dry counties and communities in the state by the time statewide prohibition was placed on the ballot in 1914.

The election of 1914 featured a bitter campaign between prohibitionists and the brewing and liquor industry. Both sides were well funded and organized. Prohibitionists brought in the infamous preacher Billy Sunday, who stumped throughout the state hyping the dangers of alcohol and extolling the virtues of life without it. Wets brought in Clarence Darrow, who highlighted the importance of free choice and reasonable laws. In the end, a high turnout by newly enfranchised women won the day, and statewide prohibition passed by a margin of roughly thirty-six thousand votes. Initial returns in Multnomah County showed the measure failing, but it wound up passing by a few hundred votes out of more than seventy-two thousand cast.

Estimates suggest that 75 percent of women who voted chose prohibition. Oregon went dry on January 1, 1916. When the state voted on national Prohibition eleven months later, Multnomah County rejected the idea by nearly ten thousand votes. But most of rural Oregon voted the other way, and the state jumped on the Eighteenth Amendment bandwagon by about three thousand votes.

It was probably just as well that Henry Weinhard didn't live to see state or national Prohibition. He died in September 1904, just months after the local option was passed by Oregon voters. The reins of Weinhard Brewing passed down to the founder's son-in-law, Paul Wessinger. Of the five children born to Henry and Louise Weinhard, only two daughters had survived: Anna and Louisa. Paul Wessinger married Anna Weinhard in 1885. The other daughter, Louise, married Henry Wagner. Wessinger and Wagner both worked alongside their father-in-law at the Weinhard Brewery before his death. Wessinger became president of the company upon his father-in-law's death and held that position until his own death in 1926.

Wessinger's first order of business was the Lewis & Clark Centennial Exposition, which was set to run from June 1 to October 15, 1905, in Portland. The Weinhard Brewery had been heavily involved in planning the event. Wessinger was one of fifteen event directors and headed up the Grounds and Building Committee. One of the Weinhard Brewery's significant contributions to the exposition was a German restaurant called the Bismarck Café, which was custom-built by a St. Louis company. As if to foreshadow the one-off beers that would become popular one hundred years later, Weinhard Brewing produced a dark lager called Kaiser Beer for the café. The beer received positive reviews and was awarded a gold medal by event judges. Weinhard also won gold medals for Columbia Lager and Export Lager. Due to the positive response to Kaiser Beer, a bottled version known as Kaiserblume was introduced in 1906. Kaiserblume and Columbia lager became Weinhard's primary brands in 1913, available on draft and in bottles.

Weinhard's export business continued to be healthy and actually benefited from unfortunate events in California, where the 1906 earthquake and fire decimated San Francisco. As a result, Northwest brewers received huge beer orders. Several Northwest breweries, including Weinhard, had been shipping barrels of beer to be bottled in San Francisco for some time. Following the earthquake and fire, Olympia Brewing decided to turn its Bay Area bottling facility into a brewery. But Weinhard Brewing did not own the plant where its beer was bottled and did not wish to build a brewery in San Francisco. So it waited for the old bottling plant to be rebuilt and promptly bought it.

This tip tray is from the Bismarck Café, constructed for the 1905 Centennial Exposition. *Courtesy of Bryan Anderson.*

The primary brand packaged for the San Francisco market was apparently Rheingold or Gold Seal. Rheingold was also available in bottles around the Northwest until 1913, when it became draft only.

Back in Portland, the Weinhard name was running into trouble due to its saloon affiliations. A fifteen-member vice commission began investigating moral decay and corruption within the city in August 1911. In a series of reports, the commission revealed 431 properties described as being "totally given over to immorality" and noted that many of the properties were owned by people of means and rented to houses of prostitution at enormous

Branded matchboxes were common promotional pieces in pre-Prohibition saloons. *Courtesy of Bryan Anderson.*

profit. Little was being done to enforce laws, the report noted, because wealthy property owners preferred that laws not be enforced. This arrangement had been going on for several decades, at least, and there was wide support for cleaning it up. Weinhard's Brewery was one of many businesses named as an accessory and promoter of vice. The end result was the Tin Plate Law, which required owners of hotels, rooming houses and saloons to maintain a sign (or tin plate) with the owner's name and address in a conspicuous spot. Many property owners devised creative ways to shield their identities. New shell companies were quickly set up, and some plates went up in foreign languages. The city was not amused. Faced with fines of up to $100 per day from noncompliance, most property owners complied. The Weinhard Brewery terminated relationships with several saloons to protect its name.

Despite the coming of the local option in 1904 and the women's vote in 1912, Portland breweries were caught flatfooted by statewide prohibition. Paul Wessinger had been president of Weinhard Brewing for ten years in the lead up to the election of 1914 and had essentially no vision for a future without beer. "A brewery is built for only one purpose, and that purpose is to make beer," he told the *Oregonian*. "We know the plants are good for nothing else." Some suggested the idea of dismantling breweries and moving to California, which remained wet until national Prohibition came in 1920. The bottom line is that most breweries, including Henry Weinhard's, expected to close if state prohibition was approved. When the final vote revealed that state prohibition was reality, Wessinger had just over a year to figure out what to do with the brewery.

WEINHARD REINVENTS ITSELF TO SURVIVE

The problem for the small Oregon breweries, and there weren't a lot of them by 1916, is that they could not afford to wait while the mistake was undone. When Oregon went dry on January 1, 1916, the state's brewing industry collapsed. Saloons closed or were converted to other businesses. Most places that closed never reopened.

To survive what it hoped and expected would be a short-lived dry spell, Weinhard Brewing reinvented itself. Its name was changed to the "Henry Weinhard Plant," and the company engaged in the production and sale of soda fountain beverages and supplies, fruit drinks (Appo and Toko), syrups, ginger ale, near beer (Luxo), mixers (Lime Rickey) and other drinks. Under Wessinger's leadership, Weinhard bought Puritan Manufacturing, gaining the rights to manufacture a collection of nonalcoholic drinks that included Ras-Porter, Graport, Loganport and Cherriport. The naming scheme was intended to remind customers of the company's brewing past, surely for future reference. Weinhard extended its reach into other areas, as well.

A cursory review of invoices from the 1920s reveals that the company was making and selling cabinets for pastries, counters, chairs and stools, wall cases and more. This was not a new focus. The company had been providing similar services to saloons before prohibition. Sales representatives now hawked hardware and fountain accessories throughout the Northwest and California. You do what you have to in bad times.

With no beer to sell, Blitz-Weinhard sold all manner of fountain-related hardware throughout the 1920s. *Courtesy of Donna McCoy.*

Possibly the most universal flaw in the thinking of those involved in the manufacture of alcohol was that Prohibition was a mistake that would not last. This was true of state and national Prohibition. Portlanders quickly decided that state prohibition was a massive mistake, despite the well-publicized problems with corruption and immorality in the saloon and hotel trade. How else do we account for the ten-thousand-vote drubbing incurred by national Prohibition in November 1916, just eleven months after state prohibition descended on the city? The state approved the idea, anyway, because Multnomah County did not yet have the population to overrule rural Oregon. Portlanders were plainly fed up with prohibition laws long before national Prohibition took effect on January 16, 1920. The same was true of many American cities, where attitudes came to affect enforcement.

One of the items that helped Weinhard and others, including Arnold Blitz and Portland Brewing, survive was malt extract syrup. This was easy for the former breweries to produce. All they had to do was mash the barley as usual and evaporate the excess water, leaving thick syrup. This product was ostensibly for baking, and many containers included recipes for cookies and such. Containers also included messages warning consumers not to add yeast, since that would result in alcohol. Anheuser-Busch took the extract game a step further by producing pre-hopped malt extract. This soon became a way for people to continue enjoying beer. Malt shops popped up everywhere. You could get a can of malt, mix it with water, add yeast and soon you would have beer. Homebrewing became popular nationwide, including in Oregon. But the end result was often crude and not very tasty. Portland's own esteemed beer writer and historian Fred Eckhardt experienced prohibition-era homebrew firsthand and had this to say about it during the 2010 program at the Bagdad Theater:

> *The homebrew was quite bad in those days. My stepfather brewed with extract syrup and sugar and water. There was no boiling. Once I knocked over a bottle of beer in his stash. It tasted like hell. Later when I was teaching winemaking, I discovered there was a great recipe for beer using wine making equipment. If they'd had decent beer making stuff in 1919, Prohibition wouldn't have mattered. But the homebrew stuff was crap.*

Setting aside the question of homebrew quality, the overriding problem with Prohibition was simple: it was a dismal failure from the start. People who wanted to drink ignored the law. Where there was demand for a product, there was a supply. This was just as true in Portland as it was across the country. The experiment led to rampant corruption and haphazard, uneven enforcement. Portland's version of it wasn't pretty, although it may have done as good a job at enforcing prohibition laws as any American city. We might know more about the efficiency of the police department during the Prohibition era, but the city didn't bother to keep crime statistics. We do know some things. When crime was expected to be high in the fall and winter, relief officers were called to duty. Suspicious characters were picked up off the street and brought in for questioning and fingerprinting. Shotgun squads guarded bank and payroll transfers.

With respect to liquor, Portland law enforcement had its issues. Homebrewed and bootlegged beer was the least of the city's problems. The more serious problem was whiskey brought in from Canada. Portland became a distribution hub for Canadian and moonshine liquor. Supplying an estimated one hundred speakeasies and one hundred beer and wine parlors demanded a steady flow of liquor. Speedboats moved contraband up the Columbia River to drop-off points on Sauvie Island with little interference. Police efforts to hinder bootlegging led to occasional confiscations. For 1923, confiscated items included 3,227 quarts of beer, 160 gallons of hard cider, 17,572 gallons of mash, ninety-two stills, 18,695 pints of whiskey and 14,141 gallons of wine. This was regarded as a mere fraction of the illicit alcohol moving through the city. Clearly, Portland was not onboard with the spirit of Prohibition, similar to many cities.

Probably the most significant impact of Prohibition, and the reason Americans eventually decided that it wasn't viable, was rampant corruption. This was a fact around the country and in Oregon. Many of Portland's speakeasies paid upward of $100,000 per month for police protection. This money was spread around widely. Patrolmen on the street received about $10 per month, good money in those days, according to local historian E. Kimbark MacColl. The real money went to higher-ups in the police department and city government. Those who didn't pay for protection, most often poor working folks, were susceptible to arrest and prosecution. There was a gigantic double standard when it came to consumption, as well. The basement of the police station on Oak Street became a sort of wholesale liquor warehouse. Liquor confiscated in raids was sold or given to city officials. In one case, a police officer was ordered to deliver whiskey to a city commissioner at his summer home on Mount Hood. Corruption and hypocrisy were the order of the day.

By the late 1920s, Americans were disgusted with what they saw. Violent crime had increased significantly, and enforcing Prohibition laws was proving impossible. Liquor was everywhere. When Democrat Al Smith ran for president as a wet candidate in 1928, many thought they could see the light at the end of the Prohibition tunnel. But it was not to be. Smith was trounced. Herbert Hoover, who spent part of his boyhood in Newberg, about twenty-five miles from Portland, won all but eight states, six of them in the Deep South. He won Oregon by a landslide of more than 100,000 votes, breaking records set by Harding and Coolidge. Even discontented Multnomah County went for Hoover by more than 10,000 votes. Some have interpreted this as a positive referendum on Prohibition, but it was more likely a referendum on Smith's Catholicism. The nation was not yet ready for a Catholic president and would not be for thirty-two years. Support for the catastrophe of Prohibition was another matter. Four years later, in the grip of the Great Depression, attitudes changed dramatically.

CHAPTER 4

REPEAL

HAPPY DAYS ARE HERE AGAIN

I need not point out to you that general encouragement of lawlessness has resulted;
that corruption, hypocrisy, crime and disorder have emerged, and that instead of
restricting, we have extended the spread of intemperance.
—Franklin Roosevelt in a 1932 campaign speech

Following the stock market crash in 1929, the United States economy went into a tailspin from which it did not fully recover until World War II. The so-called Roaring Twenties were just a memory by 1930. Resistance to Prohibition continued to grow, helped along by the fact that Americans were forced to consider the economic impact of the law. The economy needed a shot in the arm, and alcohol might provide it. Finally, the country was squandering huge amounts of money trying to enforce an unenforceable law. Voters across the nation and in Oregon had stayed on the Republican bandwagon in the decent economic times of 1928, but the Great Depression changed everything. Attitudes shifted dramatically by 1932. The coming changes would have significant meaning for the brewing industry. Portland was ready.

Democrat Franklin D. Roosevelt ran for president on a wet platform calling for repeal of the Eighteenth Amendment in 1932. Given the state of the economy, Roosevelt may well have won the election as a wet or dry candidate. Hoover was going to be out of a job, regardless of the wet issue. When ballots were counted, Roosevelt carried all but six states, winning the popular vote by more than 7 million votes and the Electoral College by a wide margin (472 to 59).

It was quite a thrashing. The story in Oregon was similar, as Roosevelt won by more than 75,000 votes out of roughly 350,000 cast. Portland and Multnomah County went to Roosevelt by more than 31,000 votes. Just as important, the people of Oregon voted to repeal state prohibition by nearly 70,000 votes. Multnomah Country accounted for a large share of the majority, voting to dump statewide prohibition by more than 40,000 votes.

The battle to end the noble experiment wasn't over. To fully end Prohibition, the Eighteenth Amendment would have to be repealed. Prior to Roosevelt taking office in March 1933 (the five-month time lag between the election and inauguration was standard until 1941), Congress convened and passed the Twenty-first Amendment, which repealed Prohibition. But nothing would change until the amendment was ratified by three-fourths of the forty-eight states, and some feared that might take years. As it turned out, ratification was not a lengthy process. For the first and only time in U.S. history, Congress directed that state ratifying conventions made up of citizens be convened

Beaver State Beer was brewed by Rose City Brewing, which operated from 1934 to 1940. *Courtesy of Bryan Anderson.*

to vote on ratification. Every other amendment in history has been reviewed by state legislatures. By choosing the alternative route, Congress hoped to avoid the conflicts and delays that would invariably occur because lawmakers were fearful of the temperance lobby. Oregon was the seventeenth state to ratify the Twenty-first Amendment on August 7, 1933. Prohibition officially ended on December 5 when Utah became the thirty-sixth state to ratify.

The more immediate solution to Prohibition came in the form of a bill sponsored by Representatives Thomas Cullen of New York and Pat Harrison of Mississippi. Perhaps foreshadowing the popularity of light beer decades later, the Cullen Bill legalized the production and sale of beer (and wine) with an alcohol content of no more than 3.2 percent by weight. Congress passed the bill on March 21, and Roosevelt signed it into law the following day. The law was set to take effect at midnight on April 7, 1933. The time applied to Eastern Time, but it appears Oregon stuck to midnight local time. Some states still had to undo state and local laws before any type of alcohol could be sold. In Oregon, where state prohibition had already been squashed, some communities still had local option laws that had to be addressed. But Portland was in the clear. The state's citizens and brewers marked their calendars and prepped for the big party.

Portland's largest breweries, Henry Weinhard and Portland Brewing, had done little more than survive prohibition. Losses were no less than $10,000 per year. Selling syrups, sodas, near beers, cereals and fountain hardware had not proven to be as lucrative as beer. Anticipating the end of Prohibition and looking to get a running start, the two breweries jumped the gun and merged in 1928. Arnold Blitz, owner of Portland Brewing, was named president of the new company, Blitz-Weinhard Brewing. Some may wonder how Blitz, whose company was significantly smaller than Weinhard Brewing, could come in and take over. Money is likely the answer. Blitz had married into the Rothschild fortune in 1910 and had the capital for needed improvements and upgrades required to meet the coming demand for beer. There's also the fact that Paul Wessinger had passed away the previous year and Blitz had more experience than Wessinger's son, Henry. Blitz would serve as president until 1940.

As "New Beers Eve" approached, Blitz-Weinhard and other Oregon brewers were woefully unprepared to meet the demand. Blitz had spent lavishly on improvements to the old facility on Upshur, but time was a problem. The company had expected a bit more lead time between when the Cullen Bill was signed and when it became law. Two weeks was not enough time to brew enough beer to satisfy thirsty palates. Shortages were expected,

Wooden kegs were still in common use in the years after Prohibition, and many had seen better days. *Courtesy of Donna McCoy.*

despite the fact that only restaurants and grocery stores with the appropriate license could sell beer initially. When the day came, thirsty Portlanders consumed every drop of beer available, although many restaurants that had never handled alcohol watched from the sideline. Blitz-Weinhard was tapped out and unable to fill any orders for two weeks. The good news was there were no arrests for drunkenness on the big day.

The beer served on April 7 was an amber lager. At 3.2 percent by weight, it was lighter in body, if not color, than the beer Henry Weinhard had been producing thirty years earlier. Breweries had brewed near beer with less than 1.0 percent alcohol during prohibition. That beer was often spiked with alcohol (from a syringe) at speakeasies and known as "needled beer." Making 3.2 percent beer was a simple process because fermentation did not have to be halted, as was the case with 1 percent brew. Despite the fact that many Oregonians had ignored Prohibition and consumed illicit alcohol, the 3.2 percent lager seemed to satisfy thirsty drinkers who hadn't had commercially brewed beer for seventeen years. It has been argued that Americans forgot what real beer tasted like during Prohibition and were fine with lighter, less hoppy brews. As we shall see, that was to be the trend going forward.

The return of legal beer brought other challenges. One restaurant worker, rusty from the seventeen-year layoff, botched the tapping of a keg and spilled its contents. A backup keg saved the day. Kegs themselves would soon prove to be a problem. As Blitz-Weinhard began to ramp up production, it soon came to the attention of authorities that some kegs did not hold the appropriate amount of beer. Until the 1950s, kegs were mostly made of wood, lined with pitch or tar to prevent beer from coming into contact with the wood. Good stuff. It turned out some kegs rendered idle by Prohibition had shrunk. Arnold Blitz explained the situation to the *Oregonian* in October 1933:

> *With the return of legal beer, we were forced to use our reserve supply of kegs and possibly 4 or 5 percent of these kegs were short measure because of long disuse. The shrinkage was brought to our attention some time ago and we immediately took it up with government officials…This situation is not peculiar to our plant, but has been met by every old-time brewing company with the resumption of the beer trade. If the matter comes into the courts, we have been promised aid from government experts.*

Sales may have been great initially, but beer production didn't return to turn-of-the-century levels for many years. The beer industry throughout the United States was seriously damaged by Prohibition, and Blitz-Weinhard was no exception. Output reached 49,000 barrels a year by the late 1930s, roughly half what it was brewing in 1900 (by contrast, Anheuser-Busch brewed nearly 2.5 million barrels that year). It took the newly formed Blitz-Weinhard about twenty years to recover from Prohibition. During this time, it continued to produce a variety of soft drinks and syrups. The arrangement for this production is worth nothing. The old Weinhard Brewery on Burnside had been replaced by a newer facility on Burnside and Northwest Couch in 1908. Following the 1928 merger, most beer production moved to the former Portland Brewing plant on Upshur. Soft drinks and syrups were produced at the Weinhard plant, which also served as the bottling plant. After improvements, all production returned to the Burnside facility in the late 1930s, and the brewery on Upshur eventually closed.

In a move intended to improve quality and efficiency, Blitz and several others (including Peter Schmidt of Olympia Brewing and Emil Sick of Rainier Brewing) formed Great Western Malting in 1935. Located across the Columbia River in Vancouver, Great Western's purpose was to produce consistent, quality malt for breweries. Up until that time, grains were malted in breweries, a time-consuming and inexact process. The men who established Great Western Malting figured that malted grain would be in high demand in the years after Prohibition and wanted to make sure they had plenty of it. The company was reorganized in 1964, and management bought the brewing interests out of the business. Today, Great Western has malting plants in Vancouver and Pocatello, Idaho, as well as distribution hubs around the country. The company has customers throughout the world and enjoys a reputation for producing high-quality product. Great Western was one of several elements that played pivotal roles in the craft revolution of the 1980s.

The fact that Blitz-Weinhard was well positioned to take advantage of the post-Prohibition demand for beer did not necessarily dissuade others from trying to capture some part of the Portland market. Improved technology and transportation networks had given the national brands better access to Oregon by the mid-1930s. Breweries that were left after Prohibition, including Blitz-Weinhard, were able to leverage their competitive advantage partially because smaller brewers had closed. This led to consolidation and larger breweries. One might argue that Prohibition killed competition in the brewing industry and essentially started the dive toward greater consolidation. But there were a number of factors involved in that process, and we will get to them shortly.

One of the more colorful outfits that attempted to enter the Portland beer market in the immediate wake of Prohibition was Northwest Brewing, owned by bootlegger Peter Marinoff of Seattle. Marinoff was involved in the production of near beer in Washington from 1925 to 1928. Sensing the end of prohibition in 1931, he started buying up breweries and soon had operations in Walla Walla and Tacoma. Then, in April 1933, Marinoff purchased the long-defunct Gambrinus Plant in Northwest Portland. He announced plans to reestablish a brewery on the property and move his executive offices there. Northwest Brewing had acquired the rights to produce Gambrinus beer and also planned to sell its own Marinoff brand. Part of the company's marketing plan involved selling beer in sealed half-gallon jugs, which apparently went over quite well.

Whatever early successes Northwest Brewing enjoyed soon unraveled. The company was charged with unfair business practices in the summer of 1933. That was just the beginning. By September, Marinoff's company was embroiled in a labor dispute over who should drive its delivery trucks. Labor disputes were an ongoing fact of life in 1930s Portland and are well documented in the pages of the *Oregonian*. In the case of Northwest Brewing, the brewery workers' union drove the trucks and claimed to have the right to

An ongoing feud with Teamsters led Northwest Brewing to put armed guards on its delivery trucks. *Courtesy of Bryan Anderson.*

do so. Teamsters argued they should be driving the trucks and picketed the Northwest Brewing plant. The dispute soon spread to businesses that sold Marinoff products. A stink bomb interrupted a performance at a downtown beergarden, and windows were smashed in taverns and stores that sold Marinoff beer. Northwest trucks were followed and harassed by Teamsters. The dispute dragged on for months. In May 1935, a flurry of violent incidents in which drivers and police were beaten put a sort of exclamation point on the seriousness of the matter. Perhaps the highlight (or lowlight) was when a dynamite bomb exploded outside William Fuegy's Rock Creek Tavern in Hillsboro. The explosion did little damage, but left a large crater that remains to this day.

Marinoff's labor troubles got personal when he was named as one of four codefendants in the case of a Teamster killed in Tacoma in May 1935. The codefendants were essentially bodyguards, and one of them shot the Teamster during an altercation. Marinoff, initially charged with murder, was eventually convicted of manslaughter and sentenced to twenty years in prison. But the conviction was overturned by the state Supreme Court, and he was released in August 1936. Teamsters considered this an affront to justice and vowed to get Marinoff, who feared for his life and fled to California. The facility in Portland, which appears to have been nothing more than a distribution center for beer brewed in Washington, was eventually closed, along with the rest of Northwest Brewing's operations. It was almost fun while it lasted.

The Marinoff situation was not the last Portland would hear from Teamsters intent on controlling the most lucrative legal and illegal operations in town. When the American Federation of Labor (AFL) granted Teamsters authority to drive beer delivery trucks in 1937, the Brewery Workers Union refused to cooperate. This led to a Teamster delivery strike against union-produced beer targeting breweries and (mainly) stores. If a store sold union-produced "red label" beer, Teamsters would not deliver nonunion "white label" beer. Teamster operatives followed union delivery trucks and warned store owners of possible trouble if they continued to stock and sell "red label" beer. The strike crippled grocery store beer sales and disrupted delivery of other goods. Strapped owners eventually came around to the Teamster point of view. By the 1950s, Teamster corruption in Portland was epidemic. It abated only after a series of investigations by the *Oregonian* brought federal authorities to town, although this is far outside the scope of this story.

Getting back to the beer, it seems likely that there would have been more competition for Blitz-Weinhard in post-Prohibition Portland had it not been for changes to the industry at large. Packaged beer was becoming increasingly popular. This was partly due to a paradigm shift in which Americans preferred to stay out of saloons and taverns and consume beer at home. At the dawn of better days in 1935, packaged beer accounted for 30 percent of beer sales (versus 70 percent draft). By 1940, the packaged number had hit 52 percent and continued to grow, reaching 88 percent by 1975. This development, helped along by better packaging and transportation, made it increasingly difficult for small breweries to enter or survive the market. Competing with established, capitalized brewing operations was simply too costly. Blitz-Weinhard, while it may have staggered through the Prohibition years, was positioned to dominate its market in the aftermath. This helped the company stifle local challenges and fend off encroaching national brands for a time.

It is almost certainly the case that Blitz-Weinhard paralleled the national brand experience during Prohibition. Distributing bottled soft drinks, near beer and related products provided insights into the importance of proper packaging and an efficient retail delivery system. Now that controlling partnerships with saloons was fully illegal, it was clear that informed retail distribution was going to be a key to success. Understanding these nuances enabled the national brands to expand dramatically in the years following Prohibition, thanks to weak or nonexistent competition. Blitz-Weinhard would never have the economy of scale necessary to compete at the national level, but it successfully applied similar concepts to Portland and the Northwest.

When Henry Wessinger, grandson of Henry Weinhard, took over as president of Blitz-Weinhard in 1940, he launched a renewal program aimed at expanding and modernizing the company. The old Blitz plant on Upshur was shut down, and the building leased to a Seattle-based winery. All production activities shifted to updated facilities on Burnside. In 1941, the company constructed a gigantic neon sign carrying the message, "Blitz-Weinhard Fine Beer Since 1856." That message stayed lit while an animation showed a tap opening and liquid flowing into a glass that foamed over. At seventy-five feet high with more than one thousand feet of neon tubing, the sign consumed massive amounts of electricity. The sign was initially located on top of the Rothschild Building at Burnside and Broadway, where it could be seen by passing motorists and throughout much of downtown. It was later moved to the top of the brewery when traffic patterns changed. Large neon signs were common in those days. Panoramic pictures of Portland show Rainier and Olympia signs on building tops in Blitz-Weinhard's town.

The coming of World War II gave Portland's economy a welcome boost. Shipbuilding yards in north Portland and Vancouver that manufactured Liberty and Victory ships provided opportunities for resident workers and migrants. The city's population grew by nearly 70,000 (to 373,000) between 1940 and 1950. U.S. per capita beer consumption, which had been flat in the years immediately following prohibition, reached 1915 levels in 1945. This happened despite the fact that breweries, including Blitz-Weinhard, agreed to reserve 15 percent of their production for the armed forces. To bolster the war effort, Blitz financed regular advertisements pointing to the importance of victory gardens and saving money and suggested that buying beer in quart bottles was good for America. Nonetheless, beer shortages were a fact of life in Portland during and even after war. It wasn't unusual for people to be waiting outside a tavern or store for the day's delivery. Regular print ads in the *Oregonian* emphasized that Blitz-Weinhard beer was worth waiting for. Whether that claim was valid is a topic for further discussion and consternation.

These were relatively good times for the Blitz-Weinhard enterprise. However, there were challenges. In 1942, the Federal Trade Commission included Blitz-Weinhard on a long list of western brewers charged with price fixing. The brewers were essentially accused of fixing the prices and terms of sale to distributors and retailers. Oregon brewers, including Blitz, vehemently denied violating any laws. In fact, Oregon laws required brewers to abide by terms considered unlawful by the FTC. Brewers demanded that the accusations be brought to trial. After procrastination on the part of the FTC, the brewers agreed to plead *nolo contendere* (no admission of guilt) and pay $250 fines. That was far cheaper than the expense of lengthy trials. Similar charges were filed against twenty-six brewers, including Blitz-Weinhard, Rainier and Olympia, in 1949. This apparently had no impact in Oregon, other than negative PR.

CHAPTER 5

LONG SHADOW

BLITZ-WEINHARD'S DECLINE AND LEGACY

You can't be a real country unless you have a beer and an airline. It helps if you have some kind of football team or some nuclear weapons, but at the very least you need a beer.

—Frank Zappa

Blitz-Weinhard enjoyed good success in the years following World War II. Per capita beer consumption had rebounded by 1945 then declined slightly by 1950 and continued flat until baby boomers gave it a bump in the 1970s. The major national brewers were in the process of leveraging advantages set in motion before and during the war.

The rule requiring brewers to withhold 15 percent of their production to supply the armed forces with beer worked to the advantage of the big brands. They brewed so much beer that the smaller regional breweries, like Blitz-Weinhard, were largely locked out of the chance to build brand loyalty among young men, their primary future customers. This led to further dominance of the national brands during the 1950s and beyond, as boatloads of disposable cash enabled them to expand and upgrade facilities and spend lavishly on national advertising campaigns. These realities led to consolidation that eventually reduced the number of breweries to just a handful, with dire consequences for regional and local breweries. Perhaps worst of all, beer itself became a casualty, marginalized into something very different than what Henry Weinhard and other pioneers had once brewed. These factors would one day coalesce with others to help launch the craft revolution. But not yet.

Just to show that temperance ideas were not completely dead in Oregon, the Oregon Anti-Liquor League sought to have more than twenty public school teachers suspended for consuming beer during a chamber of commerce–sponsored tour of the Blitz-Weinhard brewery in 1951. The tour was part of a cooperative program between the Portland School District and the chamber of commerce in which some two thousand teachers toured key businesses around the city. There were no students on the tour. At Blitz-Weinhard, some teachers had consumed complimentary beer with lunch, attracting the attention of the Anti-Liquor League. In the end, the school district and business leaders launched a counteroffensive, and nothing came of the demands. Portland had made progress since 1916.

Blitz-Weinhard was the only brewery left in Oregon after Sick's Brewing closed its Salem plant in 1953. In its marketing materials, Blitz leaned heavily on the claim of being the oldest continuously operated brewery in the West. That was an honest claim, but it did not change the fact that encroachment of the national brands was bending the rules of the game across the country. Anheuser-Busch and Schlitz were the two dominant national brands throughout the 1950s. After 1956, Anheuser-Busch had a lock on the top spot and eventually controlled more than 55 percent of the U.S. beer market by 2002. Industry analysts Victor and Carol Tremblay have suggested that "the lone constant in the post–World War II brewing industry has been the continued success of Anheuser-Busch." There's actually more to it than that, though.

Beginning in years following prohibition, American beers started to get lighter. The lager brewed by German pioneers in the late nineteenth and early twentieth centuries had been a robust brew made mostly with malted barley, hops, yeast and water. It was an honest, quality product. After prohibition, the quantity of ingredients used to brew a barrel of beer began to decline. Between 1950 and 2000, the amount of malt, adjuncts (corn, rice and so on) and hops used to produce a thirty-one-gallon barrel dropped from forty-five to thirty-five pounds. The result was lighter and lighter beers—industrial lager, if you will.

Alcohol content declined, as well. About 99 percent of brands had 6 percent alcohol before World War II; by 1996, the average domestic beer contained 4.6 percent. It is not entirely clear when Blitz-Weinhard crossed the line into industrial beer, but the evidence suggests its beer was as light as anything produced by the major brands by the 1950s. More likely, Blitz was producing lighter lagers by the late '30s. The public was certainly aware of the move to lighter beers, and not everyone was happy about it. Rose City

Brewing, one of Blitz's few competitors after Prohibition, advertised Beaver State Beer as being "made with 100 percent malt" in the late 1930s. Rose City operated from 1934 to 1940.

There has been much discussion about why light beers became popular. One thing we know for sure is the move to light beer didn't happen because it was cheaper. Total cost per barrel (material and labor) rose from about fifty-five dollars in 1950 to seventy dollars in 1970. It then dropped during the early 1980s, thanks to baby boomer–driven per capita beer consumption, before rising again in about 1985. Part of the explanation was a national trend toward processed, packaged and convenient foods. Historian and author Maureen Ogle suggested that Americans born in the 1920s and 1930s were raised on a blander, sweeter diet than their parents. When these kids reached adulthood, they rejected the idea of rich, self-prepared foods and drinks in favor of things that were lighter. Beer was a casualty. The public wanted a less malty, less hoppy version of the lager that had been popular fifty years earlier. Some part of this preference may be related to the fact that the Prohibition generation had no point of reference when it came to beer. To them, lighter tasted better.

The other not-to-be-ignored factor in the move toward lighter beers was advertising and the way in which the national brands sold their products. Starting in the early 1950s and continuing through the mid-'60s, the dominant brands spent massive amounts of money to advertise on billboards, in magazines and newspapers and on TV. In 1952, the big four (Anheuser-Busch, Miller, Schlitz and Pabst) accounted for 84 percent of network television revenues. Messages used imagery to convey each brand's identity. Heavily branded packaging linked ad imagery with products on store shelves at a time when, as mentioned earlier, packaged beer had overtaken draft beer in sales (72 to 28 percent in 1952). The big brewers pushed an increasingly bland, lowest-common-denominator product with a lot of money. Advertising surely helped assimilate consumers into the industrial beer fold. The success of coordinated advertising programs worked against the interests of the smaller regional breweries like Blitz-Weinhard, which lacked the capital to invest in similar campaigns or the ability to distribute its beer nationally. Blitz was forced to compete with localized advertising (relying heavily on print) and products that, like it or not, piggy-backed on what the national brands were doing.

By the time Blitz-Weinhard celebrated its centennial in 1956, the number of operating breweries in the United States had declined to about 270. The country had lost 200 breweries since 1947, and the downward spiral

Blitz-Weinhard was celebrating one hundred years in business when this photo was taken in 1956. The view is looking west on Burnside from Eleventh Avenue. *Courtesy of Portland City Archives.*

continued through the 1980s until there were only a few left. Privately owned Blitz was one of the few remaining independent brewing entities in the country and surely wondering how it would survive in an era of buyouts and consolidation. The company lured brewmaster Max Zimmerman from Milwaukee-based Blatz in 1956. Zimmerman was brought in to refine brewing processes. He changed the brewing formula in several ways with a clear goal in mind: "The object was to produce a milder tasting, lighter beer," he told the *Oregonian.* "Most people don't like the bitterness of hops. Our aim was to get the hop character without the bitterness."

While Blitz was doing its best to pursue a mild product that would be more widely accepted, Arnold Blitz's brother-in-law, J.M. Rothschild, was named president. As part of the centennial celebration in 1956, Rothschild buried a time capsule on the Blitz property to be opened on the brewery's bicentennial in 2056. Rothschild's tenure as president was brief. In 1958, he became chairman of the board, replacing Henry Wessinger (who retired from active management). William Wessinger took over as president and Fred Wessinger moved into the newly created role of vice-president and general manager. Bill Blitz, son of Arnold, was named executive vice-president. The Wessingers were great-grandsons of Henry Weinhard and would lead the company through the '60s and '70s. Blitz-Weinhard remained as it had been—very much a family affair.

It was perhaps a precursor of future hard times when Blitz-Weinhard's giant neon sign overlooking downtown was toppled and demolished by the Columbus Day storm of October 1962. It was not replaced. The demise of the sign notwithstanding, the company recorded steady growth and underwent several expansions during the 1960s. Bill Wessinger explained Blitz's strategy in a 1961 *Oregonian* interview. At the time, Blitz held 21 percent of the Oregon market, second to (believe it or not) Olympia. The Wessingers were committed to taking the top spot in Oregon while at the same time recognizing they had to expand into new markets to stay relevant in an increasingly competitive industry. Bill Wessinger explained the strategy:

> *We have already moved into Northern California and we are making our first shipments to Alaska today. But breaking a market anywhere is a tough business…In the Sacramento Valley in our first year we have managed 1 percent of the market. Still, we lost a lot of money there. This year our marketing expenses in California will be $25,000 to $30,000 more than the profit on the beer we sell there. It takes three years, we figure, to make the break-even point.*

Blitz's focus on the West served it well through the '60s. Capacity expanded to 400,000 barrels in 1964, supported by the installation of a high-speed bottling line. The company expanded again in 1968, following record sales of 462,000 barrels in 1967. By the end of the decade, Blitz-Weinhard controlled nearly one-third of the Oregon beer market. It didn't just do it with standard Blitz Beer. The Wessingers actually anticipated the market segmentation that was coming. They launched Olde English 800 Malt Liquor in the Northwest and in some national markets, and it did well in some areas. Blitz also formed the subsidiary Empire Brewing Company, which contract-brewed and marketed Bohemia Club and Champaign Velvet. Those brands had been produced by Atlantic Brewing of Spokane and had a good regional following. Blitz-Weinhard apparently occupied 50 percent of the available beer shelf space in Portland Fred Meyer stores by the late 1960s. But the good times would not last.

Despite a rash of industry failures and consolidations staring them in the face, Bill and Fred Wessinger bought out the stock of remaining Blitz and Weinhard family descendants in the early '70s. It's difficult to know what they were thinking. The company's prospects were dubious, regardless of successes in some areas. However, buying the stock gave them control to navigate tough times as they saw fit. Responding to the success of Miller Lite, Blitz introduced Alta, a low-calorie beer (eighty-eight calories versus Miller Lite's ninety-six) advertised as being brewed with "100 percent malts" (no corn, syrup or sugars, it claimed) in 1975. To the extent that it could engage in a national campaign, Blitz marketed Alta as a specialty brand alongside

BLITZ-WEINHARD'S LIGHT BEER

A tipping point for the national brands came in 1970, with Phillip Morris's purchase of Miller Brewing. Morris applied to the beer business the same strategies it had used in the cigarette industry. Heavy advertising and market segmentation (many brands marketed to specific market segments) were the key points. The aggressive launch of Miller Lite in 1973–74 signaled a new era in beer. Miller Lite wasn't the first light beer. Miller and other brands had tried it unsuccessfully in the past. Those efforts had positioned light beer as a diet drink, which didn't have much traction with the beer-drinking crowd.

Miller came to understand that Lite needed to be marketed as something other than a diet product. It (more likely its ad agency) developed the slogan, "Tastes Great, Less Filling." Leaning heavily on sports figures in national TV ads, Miller tapped into the beer-drinking male demographic and hit a home run where others had

Blitz-Weinhard's light beer, Alta, was launched in response to the success of Miller Lite. Alta captured a quarter of the light beer market in Oregon. *Courtesy of Donna McCoy.*

failed. It tasted great and was less filling, which meant you could drink more! Within several years, Miller doubled its total sales and reached number two behind Anheuser-Busch on the list of top U.S. brewers. The success of Miller Lite forced all national and regional brewers to produce and market a light beer. Some brewers had existing products and simply shifted the marketing approach. Blitz-Weinhard released Alta. The light beer battle was eventually won by Budweiser on the strength of advertising dollars (Bud Light is the world's most popular beer in 2013).

Olde English 800 Malt Liquor in markets across the country. Alta wasn't a hit nationally, but it earned a quarter of the light beer market in Oregon (1 percent of a category that owned 4 percent of the overall market).

By the mid-'70s, the Wessingers clearly sensed that playing themselves off against the increasingly powerful brands wasn't going to get them anywhere. Flagship Blitz was losing market share, and the company could not compete with the ad blitzkrieg of the major brands in the standard beer space. Ironically, the success they had seen with Olde English Malt Liquor tipped them off to a model that might work. They recognized that Olde English had succeeded largely because the malt liquor category had been abandoned or largely ignored by the national brands. That got them thinking about other products that they might launch into the same space. It was this thought process, a precursor to the coming craft revolution, that led them to the idea for Henry Weinhard's

Henry Weinhard's Private Reserve was a highly successfully foray into the super-premium market and a precursor to the craft revolution in the eyes of many. *Courtesy of Donna McCoy. Used with permission of MillerCoors, LLC.*

Private Reserve. Blitz would meet the challenge of the national brands, said Fred Wessinger, by "upgrading our product image" and developing specialty products that don't have a large national market.

Officially, Henry Weinhard's Private Reserve was developed to celebrate the Wessingers' buyout of Blitz-Weinhard. Private Reserve was launched in 1976 and did quite well. Within a few years it combined with Olde English 800 to account for 40 percent of company sales. The rest of the Blitz portfolio was a mishmash of low- and mid-level products that did not perform particularly well. Heavy advertising and a strong regional focus helped Private Reserve attain great success. The success of Private Reserve and, to a lesser extent, Olde English 800, may well have convinced the Wessingers that their most dire need was a national partner to help with the cost and logistics of a national marketing campaign for their best-performing beers. Or that this was a good time to sell while business was good. By the late '70s, Blitz was still a midget compared to the large national brands. Anheuser-Busch brewed 31.0 million barrels of beer in 1979; Blitz had a capacity of 1.2 million barrels but brewed only 585,000 in Portland.

After a fair amount of thought and reflection, the Wessingers sold Blitz-Weinhard to Pabst. The deal was officially announced on January 21, 1979. To many, it looked like a forced marriage. If the Wessingers, who continued to manage Blitz, thought that Pabst wanted them for Henry's Private Reserve, they were soon proven wrong. Blitz had planned to follow up the success of Private Reserve with Weinhard's Irish Style Light Ale in 1979. The Irish Ale was not ale, but never mind. Pabst balked at the idea. The super-premium category was alien to the company, and it wasn't interested in spending money on products it didn't understand. Instead, it latched onto the proven Olde English 800! In fact, anyone who did a cursory review of Pabst financials published in the *Oregonian* at the time of the sale should have been concerned for the future of Blitz-Weinhard. Pabst's profits had bombed from $21 million in 1977 to $11 million in 1978. Barrel sales had decreased by 600,000, more than Blitz produced. Pabst apparently did help finance improvements at Blitz-Weinhard, but the relationship was rickety. Pabst eventually suffered through five leadership changes during the three years it owned Blitz-Weinhard.

After several dysfunctional years, Pabst sold (transferred control may be more accurate) Blitz to G. Heileman Brewing of LaCrosse, Wisconsin, in 1983. Heileman had been an aggressive raider of regional breweries and Blitz found itself a target due to the volatile environment. In contrast to Pabst, the Heileman brass liked the idea of new products going into space unoccupied by the big brands. They signed off on a new Blitz product, but it wasn't Weinhard's Irish Ale. Instead, it was a dark version of Henry's Private Reserve, launched in 1983. Fred Wessinger, who had moved into the role of president some years before the sale to Pabst, told the *Oregonian*, "We've noticed that the discerning beer consumer has displayed a growing interest in various types of beers, particularly imported dark beers, in the last two or three years."

That statement is chilling given what was happening in Portland at the time. You wonder if the Wessingers had any appreciable knowledge of what was stewing in the minds of people like Kurt and Rob Widmer, Dick and Nancy Ponzi, Art Larrance, Fred Bowman, Jim Goodwin and the McMenamin brothers. Anyway, Henry's Private Reserve Dark did fairly well, and the Irish Ale was eventually released to great success in 1985. By this time, standard Blitz label brew had declined to an anemic share of the market, and the company was largely dependent on the Private Reserve brands and specialty products.

When Portland International Raceway needed to christen a new tower in July 1972, Blitz-Weinhard president Fred Wessinger obliged. *Courtesy of Portland City Archives.*

The fact that the Wessingers had caught on to something with their premium beer thinking was not enough to save Blitz from the predatory consolidation of the time. Per capita beer consumption was ticking downward by the mid-1980s, as the baby boom generation slid into middle age. The major brands recognized they had too much production capacity and not enough consumption. So they focused on consolidation and efficiency, which meant buying up regional breweries and shifting their production to larger, more efficient plants.

Blitz's marriage to Heileman lasted until 1996, and it is a bizarre story. In 1987, Heileman came under the control of Alan Bond, a flashy Australian businessman hoping to build a brewing empire. Bond financed the acquisition of G. Heileman with junk bonds. The deal saddled Heileman with $800 million in debt and forced it into bankruptcy in 1991. (For this and other misdeeds, Bond was later convicted and sentenced to several years in prison.) Three years later, Heileman was purchased by a private equity firm, which sold it to Stroh in 1996. Shortly thereafter, Stroh itself was in financial distress, losing several million dollars per quarter by the end of 1998. In early 1999, Stroh announced it would sell some of its brands, including the Blitz-Weinhard portfolio, to Miller Brewing. Other brands were sold to Pabst.

Stroh maintained control of the Blitz brewery property and allegedly looked for a buyer. But the brewery's prospects were dim. Had the Blitz plant been larger or more modern, it might have been purchased by another of the major brands and kept open. Had it been significantly smaller, it might have been turned into a craft brewery. The awkward elephant in the living room was the value of the property the brewery sat on. High-end condos and businesses were starting to pop up in the trendy Pearl District surrounding the old brewery. The location was no place for a brewery. Condos, offices and retail space seemed the more likely fit. The Blitz plant bottled its last beer in August 1999, after which the brewery closed and production moved to the former Olympia plant in Tumwater, Washington, owned by Miller. Cash-hungry Stroh subsequently sold the property to a development group for a king's ransom. After 143 years, Blitz-Weinhard was done in Portland.

What became of the Wessingers? They maintained offices in the old brewery throughout the 1980s, although their role in the company had been reduced to almost nothing by the end of the decade. They reportedly spent several days a week there, mostly administering to the affairs of the Wessinger Foundation and handling other non-brewery business. It seems they were paying for their own phone calls and other office expenses by the time they were kicked to the curb by Heileman in 1991. That's when brewery manager Bruce Oishi asked the Wessingers, great-grandsons of founder Henry Weinhard, to vacate the premises and find office space elsewhere. Heileman was, at the time, in the midst of Chapter 11 bankruptcy, with an unsustainable debt burden. "They probably thought it was time for the old guys to leave," Fred Wessinger told the *Oregonian*. The Wessingers soon rented space in the World Trade Center, where they carried on. In 1994, Fred Wessinger was involved with his son, Minott, in the founding of Great Northern Brewing Company in Whitefish, Montana.

There were countless mementos and death notices commiserating on the closing of the old brewery. Bill Wessinger called the closure "terribly disappointing." A nearby dairy farmer noted that his 150 cows would miss the spent barley, delivered by the dump truck load from the brewery and happily gobbled up. The president of Portland Brewing said Henry's Private Reserve may have been the predecessor of craft brewing in Portland. "It's the reason so many small brewers took to it," he said. Longtime Portland beer writer and author Jeff Alworth put a further spin on the importance of the Blitz-Weinhard legacy in a 2013 interview:

> *If you look at America, and you look at where craft beer is big, there was always a local/regional brewery—Pennsylvania, Wisconsin, Colorado, Oregon, Washington, even California. The willingness to try a beer that was local but different is common to all these places. This was crucial. The idea is spreading now, obviously. In the early days, Portland craft brewers would go around with their kegs, and people were willing to try it. It was local. People were familiar with the idea of local beer. Henry's Private Reserve planted the idea that good beer was worthwhile.*

Even though Blitz-Weinhard was physically gone, the long, proud tradition of local brewing and beer lived on in Portland. The craft beer movement was alive and well by the time the old brewery closed its doors for good in 1999.

CHAPTER 6

CHANGING TIMES

THE ORIGINS OF CRAFT

Karl [Ockert] was hired as a winemaker, but he had brewing training. I challenged him to produce a recipe that would work, and he created a great stout. We also tapped into the Oregon Brew Crew for help with recipes. They were excited to help us.

—Dick Ponzi

The roots of what became the craft beer movement in Portland (and Oregon) were not monolithic. People got interested and involved in beer for a variety of reasons. In some cases, they had somehow been exposed to better beer and decided to learn how to brew it for their own enjoyment. A few of those folks later became commercial brewers. Others took commercial brewing on as a challenge to do something no one else was doing (or doing well). Another thread of commonality shared by Portland's early wannabe brewers was an independent, anti-corporate streak. This was in keeping with Portland's distant and not-so-distant past. Finally, there was an element of small business entrepreneurship that came into play. Some of the early brewers actually thought that there might be money to be made in the business of beer and brewing. Banks and other financial institutions thought the idea laughable. As far as they were concerned, breweries didn't open; they closed. In time, the banksters would be proven wrong.

Americans who fought in World War II or were stationed abroad during the Cold War, particularly in Europe, were exposed to beer styles unlike anything available at home. The same thing happened to American tourists who visited the old country. The dominant beer at home was light lager. While Americans could find that style abroad, they also found a variety of beers that had bold flavor and character. They had tasted nothing similar at home.

When these Americans returned home, they searched for the beers they found so full of flavor. Their first option was imports, which could be found in limited quantities here and there, usually by the bottle. Sales of imported beer soared in the 1970s. Too often, though, consumers were disappointed to discover that imported beer was stale or skunked or that it had been tweaked to suit the American palate. Poor-quality imports drove some Americans to seek alternative options. However, imported beer did play a role in the craft revolution. A handful of Portland pubs embraced imports during the late '70s and early '80s, and this helped adjust palates for what was coming.

The alternative option that many explored was homebrewing. And this wasn't just something for the crowd that had been exposed to foreign beer. The counterculture movement of the 1960s influenced a generation of Americans to distrust government and large corporations. Many of this generation came to view the industrial lager brewed by the national brands as mass-produced, chemically enhanced crap. They developed similar ideas with respect to food. Homebrew was regarded as an artisan exercise and something that would give drinkers good vibes. It was in this environment that homebrewing became increasingly popular in the early and mid-1970s. Homebrew shops popped up everywhere, and wannabe brewers wanted to know more about how to brew good beer. Portland's F.H. Steinbart Company, founded in 1918, had survived Prohibition and was ready to assist. Others piled on.

Mike Royko, a syndicated columnist whose column appeared in newspapers across the country, wrote that he hated big beer. "I have tried them all…regardless of what label or slogan you choose, it all tastes as if the secret brewing process involves running it through a horse." Columnist Dave Barry quipped, "All other nations are drinking Ray Charles beer and we are drinking Barry Manilow." Portlander Fred Eckhardt's 1969 book *A Treatise on Lager Beer* contained some instructional content but suited the times perfectly in other ways. Eckhardt claimed American brewers had turned traditional lager into "pasteurized carbonated malt pop" and said imported beers were too often made for American taste. Maureen Ogle described Eckhardt's book as "a call to arms" for fledgling homebrewers.

There was one small problem, of course: homebrewing was against the law. It boggles the mind. This happened due to an error in the language of the statute that legalized home winemaking after repeal of Prohibition.

Beer was left out! This meant all brewers, regardless of brewing capacity, were technically required to obtain costly federal licenses and pay excise taxes on what they produced. Homebrewers couldn't afford that. As a result, they operated cautiously and didn't make a lot of noise about what they were doing. Homebrew clubs held meetings in secret, worried that federal agents might swoop down with shovels and axes and break up the party. Although warnings were sometimes issued, there is no record of enforcement against brewers who weren't trying to sell their goods. But homebrewing was growing more popular and the law needed to change.

Beginning in 1975, Congress began looking at changing the laws affecting homebrew. You have to remember that

Cartwright's inconsistent beers were served on draft and bottled during the brewery's brief existence. *Courtesy of Bryan Anderson.*

Washington, D.C., in those days, was somewhat more functional than it is in 2013. Nonetheless, it took some time to fix the law. Representative Barber Conable of New York introduced legislation to legalize homebrewing in July 1975. His bill didn't make it out of committee. Conable introduced similar legislation in 1977; this time the bill was passed by the House but stalled in the Senate. However, support for the idea was growing. In 1978, two senators proposed bills containing Conable's language. Neither passed. In the end, Senator Alan Cranston of California added the language legalizing homebrewing as an amendment to a tax bill that passed. Homebrewing was officially legalized when Jimmy Carter signed the bill in October 1978. Ironically, the bill legalizing brewpubs in Oregon seven years later passed in similar fashion (attached to another bill). Politics is often a strange business.

As soon as homebrewing was legal, it emerged from the closet. Charlie Papazian, who had been encouraging homebrewing from the shadows, formed the American Homebrewers Association (later merged with the Brewers Association) and launched *Zymurgy*, a national homebrewing newsletter (later magazine). In Portland, the Oregon Brew Crew (OBC) formed in 1979. National and local groups immediately became fountains of openly available information for brewers and potential brewers. Recipes for old styles were revived and new ones developed. Brewing collaborations, tastings and competitions became common. Anyone interested in brewing, including some who would become Portland's founding craft brewers, derived considerable inspiration from the OBC. Although it certainly helped that ingredients and fine water were readily available, Portland likely became a homebrewing hotbed for other reasons. The idea meshed perfectly with strong do-it-yourself, anti-establishment attitudes, as well as a keen preference for anything and everything local.

There is no accounting for how many avid homebrewers considered making the leap to commercial brewing. It seems likely that a good many people had dreams and lacked only the means to go into business. Not that lacking the means stopped everyone; it clearly did not. Borrowing money from a bank to launch a brewery was nearly impossible in those days, and this meant most early commercial craft brewers built their breweries by hand with scavenged hardware and with money borrowed from friends and relatives. Those interested in the idea of making and selling better beer to the masses didn't have to look far for examples. By 1980, there were two successful examples of craft brewing in Northern California.

The story of Anchor Brewing is fairly well known. Fritz Maytag, heir to the Maytag appliance fortune, became entangled with Anchor when he purchased 51 percent of the company in 1965. It was an odd match because Maytag wasn't a huge fan of Anchor's consistently poor product. Nor did he get much for his investment. The brewery was, by most accounts, a dilapidated operation that mainly featured crudely assembled equipment apparently hammered together by amateur sheet metal workers. But Maytag was rich and needed something to do. Seeking to rebuild Anchor's reputation, he hit the streets of San Francisco to drum up business for his beer. The reception he received was not warm. Shopkeepers and pub owners regularly sent him packing with unsavory remarks about Anchor's sour product. Most thought Anchor had closed years earlier, so bad was its beer. Maytag realized he would have to get serious about improving the beer if he hoped to save the brewery.

After a significant amount of study and ideas collected from industry experts, Maytag became increasingly convinced that he could produce a quality beer. He noticed during evenings on the town that people were buying a lot of expensive imported beer. Somehow a light bulb flashed on. He realized the upscale market was where he might carve out a niche. He resolved to make beer with imported two-row barley and real hops instead of hop extracts used by the big brands. In short, Maytag recognized there were customers who would pay more for a quality beer, in the same way they would pay for quality ingredients at a grocery story or a high-quality meal at a restaurant. It helped that he had the financial resources to see his idea through because Anchor didn't turn a profit until 1975. But Maytag's ideas and approach suggested to others that commercial craft brewing might be a viable enterprise.

Another fine example was Jack McAuliffe's New Albion Brewing Company. McAuliffe learned about full-bodied porters, ales and stouts while serving as a submarine antenna repairman in the U.S. Navy and stationed in Scotland. He developed a devout interest in homebrewing even before he returned home in 1968. He later took a job as an optical engineer in Sunnyvale, California, but spent most of his spare time learning everything he could about building and operating a brewery. Finding brewing equipment for a small brewery unavailable, McAuliffe resolved to make what he needed himself. He couldn't afford to locate his brewery in expensive San Francisco, so he rented property in rural Sonoma, figuring the town's exploding artisan culture might be a good place to sell his beer. He then proceeded to build his brewery. Funds were limited. Fermenters were fabricated from fifty-gallon barrels. The bottling line incorporated a goofy labeling machine that defied speed and efficiency. Despite the shortcomings, New Albion attracted devoted fans because the beers were fantastic. McAuliffe did no marketing or advertising, preferring to let his beer to the talking. New Albion eventually went under, sunk when it got trapped in a plan to dramatically expand in 1982.

Taken together, the examples set by Anchor and New Albion informed the ambitions of wannabe commercial brewers. Maytag and McAuliffe demonstrated that it was possible to brew and sell full-bodied, old-style beer made from traditional ingredients. McAuliffe proved to entrepreneurs and homebrewers that you could build a small commercial brewery without going to significant expense and that good beer would sell itself in the right setting. These concepts helped motivate a new generation of brewers and breweries in hotspots around the country. Portland would eventually become the hottest of the hot, despite or perhaps because of its climate.

After Henry Weinhard, Charles Coury may have been the most important brewer in Oregon history. And not because his brewery was a success; in fact, it was a disaster that lasted only two years. Coury, a commercial winemaker and longtime homebrewer, founded Cartwright Brewing in 1980. Cartwright was the first new brewery in Oregon since prohibition, located in the heart of what today is playfully referred to as the "Beermuda Triangle" in Southeast Portland. Coury took his experience as a homebrewer and winemaker and attempted to turn it into a commercial success, just as New Albion had done in California. The emerging Portland beer culture was rooting for Cartwright to be successful. A growing crowd of people wanted locally produced, quality beer. Unfortunately for everyone, that's not what Coury delivered.

The main problem with Coury's brewery is that he used the same sanitary values for beer as he had used in winemaking. He didn't have a heat exchanger because you didn't use heat exchangers with wine (which isn't boiled). Thus, the beer he brewed was left to cool in open containers, inviting wild yeast and infection. Large garbage bags were evidently used for fermentation. The beer often went sour after leaving the brewery. Dick and Nancy Ponzi, the owners of Ponzi Vineyards who soon founded Columbia River Brewing (later Bridgeport), derived their inspiration for wine from Coury. They wanted to see Cartwright succeed, and they helped him. "Charles didn't have the right equipment for beer," Dick Ponzi recalled. "Then he took on

The north side of the old rope factory as it stood in 1981, three years before Bridgeport Brewing opened. *Courtesy of Portland City Archives.*

bottling. He dealt with some serious handicaps. We loaned him equipment and money. Like a lot of people, we wanted to see something good happen. Obviously that's not the way it turned out."

Issues with consistency and quality led to financial problems, and Cartwright closed in late 1981. To some observers, the Portland craft beer revolution had crash-landed on takeoff. However, a few aspiring entrepreneurs perceived something different. Kurt and Rob Widmer were inspired by Coury and recognized that his failure was mainly due to technical shortcomings, not bad ideas. The Ponzis figured that Coury might have succeeded if he'd had better equipment. Mike McMenamin, who was at the time involved in the beer distribution business, sold Cartwright beer and realized it would have succeeded if it had been better. As far as the McMenamin brothers were concerned, Coury was a visionary. Given the popularity of sour beers in contemporary Portland, some have suggested that Cartwright was simply thirty years ahead of his time. Fred Eckhardt noted that "Coury was his own worst enemy. The last jolt was that his final batch was actually good beer, but it wasn't his fault. It was called Deliverance Ale, and it had gotten infected just right so that it tasted like a Belgian ale, although he hadn't meant it to."

The Ponzis were the first to take Coury's example and run with it. They looked at commercial brewing in Portland from an entrepreneurial perspective. Both understood what had happened at Cartwright and saw good beer as something that could be commercially viable if done right. Dick Ponzi took it on as a personal challenge to brew good beer. The first thing the Ponzis needed was a space, preferably somewhere cheap.

In those days, most of what is currently known as the Pearl District was occupied by broken-down warehouses and abandoned industrial buildings. Many streets were unfit to drive, walk or bike on. Potholes in the area could swallow a Volkswagen. But a large area north of Burnside was conveniently zoned for Light Industrial use, thanks largely to Blitz-Weinhard. That meant you could locate a brewery there without the need for a conditional use permit. This is where the Ponzis established their brewery, in a long-abandoned (Portland Cordage) rope factory, more recently occupied by the Pennsylvania Tire Company, on Northwest Marshall. Roger Madden owned the building. Dick Ponzi described the conversation they had about leasing space there in a 2013 interview:

We talked to Roger and told him we wanted something with some character but small. He asked what we were doing. When I told him we were opening a *brewery, he busted a gut laughing. He asked how much space we wanted, still laughing. I laid out what we wanted, and it wound up being $600 a month for something like six thousand square feet. The lease was written and signed on the back of an envelope. Roger thought we were nuts. He would have sold us the building for a million bucks, but we weren't interested in that. In retrospect, that would have been a good investment. As the business grew, Roger was pretty proud that something cool was happening in his old building. We kept expanding, and we'd ask him for help and he'd go along with it.*

The operation today known as Bridgeport Brewing did not initially go by that name. When the Ponzis were planning their brewery, they hoped to call it Portland Brewing. That would have been a sort of tip of the hat to Arnold Blitz's long-extinct brewery on Upshur, not far from the old rope factory. The Ponzis soon discovered the Portland Brewing name was not available— another group of aspiring brewers had claimed it for themselves. When the Ponzis' brewery opened in early 1984, it was called Columbia River Brewing. All the beers from the outset carried the Bridgeport name. After legislation enabled them to open a pub, it was named the Bridgeport Brewpub, and Columbia River was eventually dropped. It would reappear several decades later.

Bridgeport's Old Knucklehead barley wine was initially bottled in 1989. The face on the label has changed many times over the years. *Courtesy of Bryan Anderson.*

To supplement their knowledge of beer and brewing and get the operation off the ground, the Ponzis hired Karl Ockert, a 1983 graduate of the fermentation science program at University of California–Davis. Ockert had originally gone to Humboldt State with dreams of becoming a forest ranger. That dream collapsed when Ronald Reagan was elected president in 1980. Ockert figured a career as a forest ranger might not pan out, so he entered the program at UC–Davis. While the wine part of the program had existed for a long time, the brewing portion was quite new. Most of the students who studied winemaking didn't bother with beer. But Ockert bothered with it because he figured knowing something about beer might help him get a job after graduation. How right he was.

Ockert was ostensibly hired by the Ponzis as an assistant winemaker. It became clear from the outset that something else was afoot. "My first day on the job, Dick talked nonstop about brewing," Ockert remembered. "From July 1983 on, we schemed on how to put together a brewery. We had to use dairy equipment. No one in the United States was making small-batch brewing equipment in those days. We had to learn how to make it. I learned how to weld, how to plumb. That's the way it was. The first mash tun was a square dairy tank. Brewing was arduous. Nothing was automated." By late 1984, Columbia River Brewing was up and running. The first brewhouse had a fifteen-barrel capacity, large for its time and place, and used gentle steam heat. The first beer was Bridgeport Ale.

Not long after Columbia River (to be referred to as Bridgeport from here on out to avoid confusion) opened, Ockert got some bad news. "I heard Kurt Widmer was going to start a brewery. I thought, 'We're screwed! Portland will never support more than one brewery…why doesn't he go back to Eugene!? This is my town!'" Such was the thinking of the time. Everyone wondered how much craft beer the market would bear.

It turned out the Widmer story was true. Kurt and Rob Widmer became interested in brewing largely because they had nothing else going on. Kurt had worked for the Washington Transportation Department in a temporary job and was working for the Internal Revenue Service in the early '80s. Rob was working for a businessman who wanted to open a chain of candy stores in the Seattle area. The Widmer business plan was based on the import model. Kurt had been studying the rising popularity of imported beer and thought the premium segment could be targeted with a good local product. The brothers had been homebrewing since the late '70s, partly because Kurt had lived in Germany and thought it would be fun to replicate beers he found there. They also had an uncle who made good beer as a homebrewer and figured they might be able to do the same. However, the beers Kurt and Rob brewed were not very good. Kurt recalled the experience:

Our homebrews weren't great. The ingredients weren't very good. We used malt extract, freeze-dried yeast and cheesy hops. We were happy when the beer was drinkable. It got better when we started mashing, and people who tried it liked it because it was different. There was no point of reference at the time. I don't know what made us think we could sell our stuff. The best beers came when we got our brewery up and running. We sewered our first ten batches, but the first good one was a lot better than anything we made as homebrewers.

The original Widmer brewery opened in April 1985 and was located at Northwest Fourteenth and Lovejoy, barely a hop and a skip from Bridgeport Brewing at Northwest Thirteenth and Marshall. It had taken the brothers about nine months to put their ten-barrel brewery together. The hardware was mostly scavenged junk. Several tanks came from a nuclear power plant that failed to get licensed. The boys found them in a junkyard and paid scrap value. They got a heat exchanger that was ten times larger than what they needed and somehow made it work. Fermenters were fabricated because they had studied numerous publications and knew what they wanted. They got a lot of help from their dad, Ray, along the way. "Our dad was a farm boy and knew how to fix things," Rob said. "He was retired and not doing much, so we conned him into helping us. We often couldn't afford to go out and buy new parts. Dad could fix stuff. He figured out how to build a keg filling system."

When people think of Widmer Brothers Brewing, the first thing that typically comes to mind is Hefeweizen, which became its flagship brand a few years later. But the initial Widmer offerings were Altbier, amber-colored ale that was hoppy for its day, and Weizen, filtered wheat beer. Business was slow in the beginning, but it picked up after about eighteen months. When things did pick up, one of biggest challenges they faced was money—or the lack thereof. "We got to the point where we were growing too fast," Kurt recalled. "We had depended on used kegs early on, and eventually you couldn't find them. That forced us to buy new ones, which we couldn't afford. The price difference was huge. Used kegs were about ten dollars; new ones were eighty dollars. Finding the money to fuel our growth was a challenge."

As the first of the emerging craft breweries, Widmer and Bridgeport faced the monumental challenge of finding customers. They could not sell directly

DON YOUNGER AND THE HORSE BRASS PUB

The Horse Brass Pub occupies a seminal place in the history of craft brewing in Oregon and is a place Rose City residents and visitors must experience. Its legend is extensive. The business was purchased by the late Don Younger in 1976. What makes the story interesting is that the transaction occurred during a day and night of heavy drinking. When he discovered the bill of sale the next morning, Younger reportedly had no recollection of how it happened. He and his partner, his late brother, Bill, were no strangers to the bar business. They founded the Mad Hatter tavern in Southeast Portland in 1967 and, later, Strawberry Fields in Gresham. The beer landscape was sparse in those days.

Portland's original publican, the late Don Younger, loved great beer and promoted it tirelessly. This painting graces the hearth at Lompoc's Sidebar in Northeast Portland. *Photo by the author. Painting courtesy of John Foyston.*

At the time the Youngers took over the Horse Brass, Blitz was the only beer on tap. Of course, you could get a bottle of Olympia, Lucky Lager, Rainier or Bud if Blitz wasn't your thing. But locally brewed Blitz was Don Younger's thing, and that didn't change until, pushed by a young English bartender, he sampled a Bass Ale. He loved it. And so began his search for unique beers, which were primarily imports in the early days.

As the craft beer movement began to take off in Portland, Younger was in the middle of it. The Horse Brass, along with Carl Simpson's Dublin Pub (also located on Southeast Belmont in those days), became known as places where brewers and patrons would convene to taste and critique beers. Younger offered advice, encouragement and a place to share ideas. He not only bought and promoted their beer in his pub, but he also encouraged other pubs and retailers to give the stuff a shot.

Events like Fringe Fest, Oregon Beer Week and Oregon Craft Beer Month originated with Younger, according to local beer icons, John Foyston and Lisa Morrison. "People somehow assume that these ideas have always been out there...like craft beer," Foyston said. "But that's not the case. Someone had to think these things up, and Don was a guy who did."

Younger passed away in early 2011 and is deeply missed by the Portland beer community. But the Horse Brass carries on. It celebrated thirty-five years in business in 2011 and today has fifty-nine taps featuring a quality selection of imports and specialty beers from the Northwest and beyond. The Horse Brass is not to be missed by anyone mildly interested in fine beer, whether local residents or those from another planet or galaxy.

to customers because the law didn't allow it. Neither company had money for advertising or marketing. Yet they needed to build credibility and awareness for what they were doing. You couldn't simply walk into a bar and get a tap handle in those days. Most places had only a single brand on draft, whether it was Blitz, Bud, Pabst, Miller or otherwise. Early craft brewers had to win customers to be considered for a tap handle. The solution was to schlep kegs to local watering holes and get patrons to try the beer. This is how they built credibility until and even after it became legal to sell direct in a brewpub setting. Karl Ockert, currently technical director for the Master Brewers Association of the Americas, recalled how it worked in a 2013 interview:

> *We had no sales force or marketing budget. We'd brew all day and then go to a beer night at a pub and sample our beers. That's how it was. Most people were receptive to tasting our beers. The ones who were most receptive were those who had traveled and tasted better beers abroad. But people were starting to look for artisan options: good bread, good coffee. Good beer was part of that. Still, we were trying to sell beer no one had heard of for several times what they were paying for macro beer. It wasn't easy at first.*

A few places understood immediately what the new breweries were up to and supported them almost from the beginning. Don Younger at the Horse Brass Pub had been pouring imports for many years and jumped at the chance to serve good local beer. The Horse Brass became known as a place where brewers would come to sample one another's beers. Bill McCormick (Jake's) was one of the first accounts for Widmer and Bridgeport. Carl Simpson's Dublin Pub was

For many years, Widmer Brothers Brewing used a vintage Datsun truck for deliveries and to pick up grain and hops. In this shot, taken after they moved to Russell Street, the boys load kegs. *Courtesy of Widmer Brothers Brewing.*

another early supporter. The McMenamins helped out by putting the initial craft beers on in their pubs. It's important to note that everything was draft at this point. None of Portland's early craft breweries, outside of the failed Cartwright, had any interest in bottling initially. The model was to sell kegs to restaurants, taverns and bars. The founding craft brewers weren't intent on getting rich or famous. They simply hoped to make a decent living brewing and selling beer. They also had no inkling of what the distant future held.

Keg distribution was comical. The Widmers used an old Datsun pickup truck to deliver kegs and to pick up grains and hops. They found that they could stuff a hoard of kegs into the bed if they loaded it just right. "It was our dad's truck," Kurt Widmer recalled in a 2012 interview:

> We later made him sell it to us. We would deliver kegs to Seattle. You would fill the bed, then wedge kegs between the sides and the kegs in the middle. You could fit thirteen kegs in there! We couldn't afford freight, so we would take turns driving up to Yakima for hops or to Great Western [Malting] for grains. Stopping distance when loaded was a quarter mile. It's gone through several sets of brakes but still has the original clutch. We still put it out for special events here. Rob keeps it alive.

It's entirely possible that craft beer would have survived and become a decent business for the founding brewers and others who were waiting in the wings. But the inability to sell directly to customers would have been a continued drag on growth. Established and aspiring brewers wanted to be able to sell their beer directly to customers in a pub setting based loosely on the German model. Basically, they wanted a restaurant where beer was brewed and served and where individuals and families could come. Many of the early brewers knew of the pub model from their travels in Europe. The idea came home to roost with the knowledge that California and Washington had legalized brewpubs in the early '80s. Portland's founding brewers became convinced that getting similar legislation passed in Oregon was crucial to their future success. How right they were.

CHAPTER 7

CRUCIAL ELEMENT

THE BREWPUB REVOLUTION

We just wanted to brew our own beer to sell in our pubs…instead of buying beer from somebody else. We're stubborn Irish people, if you haven't figured that out. We like doing things ourselves.

–Brian McMenamin

The drive to pass legislation legalizing on-premise sale of beer to patrons, which became known as the Brewpub Bill (full text in Appendix I), was arguably the single most important episode in the history of Oregon brewing. There is no doubt about it. Without the bill, craft beer would have remained in the shadows of taverns and pubs, largely hidden from public view. When you have no marketing budget and your beer isn't available for purchase in grocery stores because you don't bottle, you need a means of showing off your product to the public. The brewpub provided it. When the bill finally came to fruition, craft beer in Oregon and Portland was forever changed for the better. Other promotional vehicles were invented once the industry gained a foothold. Modern Portlanders, particularly those who migrated after 1990, have really no idea how or where the city's craft beer infrastructure was born. It was the brewpub legislation.

Just because it turned out to be a good idea does not mean the law glided through the legislature. As we shall see, there were those who feared the brewpub idea and opposed it. There's also the fact that it somehow became entangled with a struggling national brand's effort to enter the Oregon market. As alluded to earlier, the Brewpub Bill was not passed as standalone legislation; its language was inserted into another bill that passed at the end of the 1985 session. For many years, most versions of the story have gotten it wrong. Even the principal players don't know or fully recollect what happened, and the story is more difficult to piece together today because some of the key players are no longer around to answer questions. The account you'll read here is based on legislative documents, interviews, newspaper reports and a bit of intuition. Honestly, the story of the Brewpub Bill could easily consume an entire book.

The reason there was a need for such a bill is that post-prohibition laws made it illegal for breweries to sell directly to customers. This was a reaction to the situation in which breweries had profited and controlled market access via their ownership of saloons and other outlets before prohibition. States made and monitored these laws. In Oregon, the three-tier system required brewers to sell their beer to a distributor, which then sold to the retailer. These laws were intended to prevent monopolies and limit consumption. They may have worked initially. However, consolidation in the brewing industry by the 1980s reached the point where the national brands were pressuring distributors to carry only their brands, exactly what the three-tier system was supposed to prevent. But never mind. When they entered the market, Widmer and Bridgeport were able to sell directly to taverns as long as they did not own or have an interest in those establishments. Tasting rooms attached to the brewery were also fine, but no beer could be sold there—a serious disadvantage.

The vision for the brewpub legislation came from several quarters. First, the brewers and prospective brewers knew full well that brewpubs already existed in California and Washington. Those states were the first to legalize brewpubs in 1982. Nothing sinister was happening as a result. It made sense that Oregon should join the fun. Then you had the Ponzis, who had been immersed in the wine industry for many years. Oregon's wine industry was far ahead of its beer industry at the time. Wineries had as their primary feature tasting rooms where patrons could also buy wine. Wine had broken the three-tier system years earlier, partly because wineries didn't have a history of owning saloons before prohibition. The Ponzis took the example of what was being done with wine and applied it to craft beer. It was a strong argument. How could anyone say that the same rules shouldn't apply to beer?

A small group of entrepreneurs resolved to get the law changed by late 1984. The group included the Ponzis, Karl Ockert, Kurt and Rob Widmer, Mike and Brian McMenamin, Art Larrance, Fred Bowman and Jim Goodwin. Bridgeport had been operating for about a year at this point, and

The Bridgeport brewers outside the entrance to the pub, circa 1989. Brewmaster Karl Ockert is at the far left. *Courtesy of Karl Ockert and Bridgeport Brewing.*

the Widmers were getting ready to open their brewery (in April 1985). The McMenamins had pubs and were interested in brewing; Larrance, Bowman and Goodwin planned to open a brewpub once the law passed. There was surely some interesting conversation about how their idea should be transformed into legislative action. Probably the first thing these folks should have come to grips with is that they were rank amateurs when it came to politics. They naïvely assumed they could draft a bill that made sense, get it introduced in the legislature and it would pass. If only.

There is a bit of entertaining legend attached to this story. As they looked for possible connections to Salem, it turned out that Larrance knew Representative Tom Mason, a Portland Democrat, via Mason's law firm (Larrance was a client). After an evening workout, Larrance approached Mason in the shower at the Multnomah Athletic Club and introduced him to the brewpub concept. Inquiring minds may wonder why the idea was presented in a shower and not an office. It seems the two men were friends and saw each other at the MAC regularly. Anyway, Mason agreed to look over the bill and eventually introduced it in the Oregon House in late January 1985 as HB 2284. He positioned the bill as an "economic development and quality of life measure."

Just over a month later, in early March, HB 2284 flew through the House by a unanimous vote of fifty-six to zero. It looked like the brewpub legislation was on cruise control and would easily pass. But that was not its fate. Instead, HB 2284 became a sort of pawn in two disputes: the first was over whether to let Coors sell its beer in Oregon; the second involved the state's beer distributors, some of which weren't sure they liked the idea of breweries selling their own beer. Some feared that it might hurt their business. These issues came to the forefront in the state Senate.

As the bill was making its way to a vote in the Senate, there were a number of hearings in front of various committees. Dick Ponzi gave extensive testimony at an April 11 hearing before the Senate Business, Housing and Finance Committee. Everything looked good. Then, during a work session on May 9, the bill was tabled. That effectively meant that it couldn't be considered again during the session. The two ringmasters that day were Senator Glenn Otto (D-Troutdale) and Senator L.B. Day (R-Salem). Newspaper and personal accounts indicate that the two senators got a kick out of demolishing the bill. Dick Ponzi recalled the day in a 2013 interview:

> We went down for a hearing, sat down and waited our turn. Day and Otto killed the bill. We got out of the meeting and are looking at each other saying, "What does it mean?" It was basically dead. We figured that was the end of it. The entire process was frustrating. People would give us promises, and we'd find out on the way home that our ideas had been tossed. We began to wonder how anything ever got done in Salem.

Otto subsequently said that he blocked the bill because he came to believe Coors would use it to get into Oregon, which would not have worked for reasons that will become evident. Day blocked it because a political ally in his district owned a beer distributor and didn't like the brewpub idea.

Coors figures in the story because, by 1985, it had been trying to tap the Oregon market for five or more years. This was a response to continuing industry consolidation and the need to tap into every available market. Coors was trying to compete with Anheuser-Busch and Miller, both of which were a good deal larger. For decades, Coors had been available in a limited number of states, creating a sort of cult-like status for its beer. The popular

'70s movie *Smokey and the Bandit*, in which Coors beer was being smuggled to a state where it wasn't available, provided a fairly accurate picture of what was going on. However, the limited availability strategy had lost steam in face of increased competition and consolidation. Coors was distributed in more than forty states by early 1985 and needed more. Oregon was one of those markets.

Coors ran into two problems. First, Oregon had a fifty-year-old statute forbidding the sale of unpasteurized beer, which was officially considered unhealthy. All Coors beer was cold filtered, not pasteurized. Second, Coors had developed a reputation for being anti-labor, anti–women's rights, anti-environment and ultra right-wing. A lot of Oregonians didn't like Coors. Nonetheless, the company wanted in and sued the Oregon Liquor Control Commission (OLCC) in September 1984. The crux of the suit, filed in Multnomah County, was that the cold filtering process used by Coors accomplished the same thing as pasteurization and that Coors' rights were being violated under the equal protection clause in the U.S. Constitution. State officials clearly agreed with Coors on cold filtering. Several years earlier, the OLCC had redefined pasteurization to include cold filtering, which it considered equal to pasteurization. But the Joint Council of Teamsters, led by none other than Senator L.B. Day, challenged that ruling and the state Court of Appeals overruled the OLCC, saying pasteurization was strictly defined and not open to interpretation. Now the matter was in court again.

While the new suit was pending, Coors operatives introduced legislation that would allow the company to sell its beer in all retail outlets in Oregon. The bill, HB 2015, was strongly opposed by Oregonians who didn't like Coors' politics or its stance on women, unions or the environment. The bill stalled. But Coors was determined this time and launched a methodical effort that included an organized letter-writing campaign targeting legislators and the media. A big part of the campaign pointed to contradictions in the law. In actual fact, Coors had been selling its beer in Oregon dating back to 1983, when it began selling kegs and packaged beer in taverns and restaurants in some parts of the state. How could it do that? Because the pasteurization law applied *only* to beer sold in retail outlets. While legislators, jurists and bureaucrats debated the finer points of cold filtering versus pasteurization, Coors did its best to make a case for hypocrisy in the law.

The loophole in the pasteurization law affected taverns and restaurants because they typically served lots of draft beer. And draft beer is universally unpasteurized, which is arguably why it tastes better. In fact, there is nothing unhealthy about draft beer. As Fred Bowman quipped in 2010, "People don't get sick drinking unpasteurized beer; they get sick drinking *too much* beer." Everyone knew there was nothing wrong with unpasteurized beer. Yet with a wink and a crooked smile, Oregon's goofy law was being used by well-placed politicians as a means of keeping Coors out of Oregon. Not for long.

Any suggestion that passage of the Brewpub Bill would somehow let Coors enter Oregon (Glenn Otto's position) was flagrantly false. All the beer produced in brewpubs would be draft beer. Coors was already selling draft beer in some Oregon taverns and had nothing to gain via passage of the Brewpub Bill. If the bill had included language allowing for the bottling and sale of unpasteurized beer, the argument might have made sense. But there was no such language. Craft brewers had no interest in bottling at that point. To them, bottling meant going out of business, as had happened with Cartwright. They weren't thinking about pasteurization. Coors' legal and legislative efforts had always been designed to get bottles and cans of cold-filtered beer into grocery stores. Its beer was doing fairly well in taverns and restaurants, but that represented less than 25 percent of the market. Coors wanted access to 100 percent of the market.

By late May, resistance to the two bills had softened somewhat. The Coors legislation was combined with the brewpub language in SB 45 on June 1, a move widely reported in the media. Various arguments against the two measures were essentially quashed during several hearings. Lobbyists for beer distributors that weren't keen on the brewpub concept advised lawmakers to let the legislation go through. It looked to the world like SB 45 would pass. This helps explain why many people connected with the legislation believe to this day that it passed as part of the Coors Bill. But that isn't what happened. On June 12, SB 45 cleared the House on a vote of forty-five to fourteen. Hours later, for reasons that are not entirely clear, the bill was blocked in the Senate. Opposition to Coors based on labor and political considerations was entrenched and unyielding.

This series of events was taking place very near the end of the 1985 legislative session, and there were concerns that time would run out. Supporters of the Brewpub Bill, it turns out, had bought a sort of insurance policy. On June 4, House representative Verner Anderson (R-Roseburg) inserted the brewpub language into SB 813, a bill that addressed the granting of liquor licenses to bed-and-breakfast establishments. In effect, there were two separate bills with the brewpub language in the legislative pipeline by early June. The Coors version failed to get through the Senate, which was still hostile to Coors. With the brewpub language amended to the B&B bill, which cleared the House and had already cleared the Senate

Portland's first brewpub, McMenamin's Hillsdale Public House and Brewery, as seen in the early 1990s. *Courtesy of McMenamins.*

in its base form, it need only go through Conference Committee for review. In a five-minute Conference Committee meeting on the afternoon of June 17, Senator L.B. Day asked several questions about what had been added since SB 813 left the Senate. He then motioned for the amendments to be accepted and the bill approved. Day's motion carried unanimously, and that was it. The Brewpub Bill headed to the governor's desk, where it was signed on July 13. Craft brewing in Oregon was forever changed.

Although it looked like Coors would once again be banned from Oregon stores, events intervened. In Portland, Circuit Court judge Bill Snouffer ruled the state pasteurization law unconstitutional on June 12. He found that "neither the safety nor the health of the people of the state is jeopardized by the consumption of unpasteurized beer." This ruling came down hours after the state Senate had voted down SB 45, the bill combining Coors access with the brewpub language. No one was quite sure what would happen next. Would the OLCC appeal Snouffer's ruling? Given the OLCC's earlier effort to amend the law, that prospect seemed doubtful. Would the Teamsters intervene? If they did, they would have to demonstrate that unpasteurized beer was unhealthy, a steep hill to climb given the amount of unpasteurized beer already being consumed in Oregon. Would lawmakers make it a moot issue by allowing Coors into the state? In the end, the legislature blinked and passed SB 50, a rewritten bill allowing Coors into Oregon, on June 19. Coors soon became available in stores around the state.

An interesting point with respect to the Brewpub Bill is that authors had inserted emergency clause language: "This act being necessary for the immediate preservation of the public peace, health and safety, an emergency is declared to exist and this Act takes effect on its passage." This was a bit over the top. In fact, the only emergency at hand was in the minds of the people who had lobbied for the bill's passage and were chomping at the bit to open brewpubs. Passage of the bill opened the door, and these folks sprinted through it.

The McMenamins were the first to take advantage of the legislation. They started brewing at their Hillsdale Pub in the fall of 1985, recognized as the first modern brewpub in Oregon. The McMenamins had different ideas about beer. They liked to collect pubs and were already doing so. They really had no great ambitions in terms of widely distributing their beer beyond their own pubs. "We weren't really sure what on-premise brewing meant at first," Brian McMenamin recalled. "Did it mean cooking beer on a stove? We knew we could use old dairy equipment. So we went down to Tillamook and found some tanks, jerry-rigged some stuff and it worked. The initial beer wasn't very good, but we had some decent stuff by 1986."

One of the reasons they had quality issues is they were using malt extract initially, via fifty-gallon drums out of California. John Harris, then an unknown, was hired to brew at the Hillsdale Pub based on his homebrewing experience. "We were using extract," he said. "Other brewers looked down on us." Harris moved to the Cornelius Pass Road House, another McMenamins property, for a while, but he returned to Hillsdale when they started mashing. "The beers got better at that point, and it was fun. We brewed with fruit, which wasn't common at the time. We had a lot of

FESTIVAL POWER

Modern festival-crazy Portland owes much of its existence to the Oregon Brewers Festival (OBF). The event is so popular that it has spawned countless beer-related events in the city. Held the last full weekend in July each year, the event attracts thousands of beer fans to Waterfront Park and is the crowning moment in Oregon Craft Beer Month. It is the largest outdoor beer festival in America.

The history of the OBF is rich. In the early days of the craft beer movement in Portland, brewers wanted an event to promote their beers. The initial beachhead came in 1987, when Papa Aldos Pizza held a Blues Festival at Waterfront Park in late July. Thinking that it would need

The original Oregon Brewers Festival poster from the first year. *Courtesy of Art Larrance.*

beer, it approached Portland Brewing about getting involved. Portland Brewing cofounder Art Larrance agreed to provide beer. He anticipated a small crowd and planned accordingly. To his surprise, the taps ran continuously once turned on. Larrance wound up making countless trips between the festival and the brewery to refill spent kegs. In the end, seventy-six kegs were consumed.

As 1988 dawned, Papa Aldos decided a blues festival wasn't quite the right demographic fit for them. But they had a two-year permit to do an event in Waterfront Park. They turned the permit over to the Blues Association, which wanted to do its festival around the Fourth of July. That left an open, permitted date in late July. Portland Brewing bought the permit from the Blues Association for $500. Larrance then got Widmer and Bridgeport involved. The McMenamins were busy with their own projects and didn't want to help organize, but they did provide beer.

The first official OBF happened in 1988. There were twenty-two breweries involved, each serving one beer. Logistical issues were rampant. The expected *crowd of five thousand tripled to fifteen thousand. The OBF continued to grow year by year. It expanded to three days, then four and finally five in 2013. Several thousand volunteers help make the event happen every year. Larrance never expected the OBF to get as big as it has, although he thought that a large, outdoor event focused on craft beer could be successful. The 2013 festival served up more than eighty-five beers in a wide range of styles and attracted more than eighty thousand beer fans. It is the quintessential event of the summer and a destination for beer lovers galaxy-wide. Any self-respecting beer fan should attend this event at least once.*

freedom to create stuff, although they would sometimes say, 'Don't make that again!'" Harris moved on to Deschutes Brewing in Bend in 1988 and was instrumental in developing iconic beers like Mirror Pond, Obsidian Stout and Black Butte Porter. He returned to Portland in 1992 to run Full Sail's brewery on the South Waterfront, a job he held for twenty years. Today, he has his own Portland gig in the works, to be called Ecliptic Brewing.

The great contribution of McMenamins' pubs was not their beer, even though it was important at the start because it offered an alternative to industrial lager. The brothers didn't follow the model of having a single large brewery for their production, although the eventual Edgefield brewery is fairly large; instead, they operated small breweries in many pubs following the English/European approach. Their beers often varied from pub to pub, a fact they happily advertised. An abundance of pubs and a willingness to pour beers produced by other brewers was their significant contribution to the craft beer revolution. Regardless of where you found yourself in Portland by the late 1980s, you could usually find a McMenamins pub with a selection of craft beer. They kept adding new locations every year and eventually built an empire. Their contribution to the success of the overall craft beer movement cannot be overstated.

After Hillsdale, Bridgeport was next to open a pub in March 1986. It was eventually a huge success, but not at the start. Bridgeport beers were always solid. Following the success of Bridgeport Ale, there was Bridgeport Stout. In 1987, Bridgeport brewed Blue Heron Pale Ale for an Autobahn Society fundraiser. Other early beers included Golden Ale, Pintail ESB, Amber, Rose City Ale, Coho Pacific Light Ale and Old Knucklehead, a beefy, seasonal barley wine. Blue Heron and Old Knucklehead were the first Bridgeport beers to be bottled in 1989. The Old Knucklehead label has always featured

Above: The term "Beervana" was first applied to Portland in this 1994 guide to the city's breweries and pubs. *Courtesy of Jane Zwinger and Willamette Week.*

Right: The Oregon Brewers Festival nearly always has a fun and colorful theme. This is one of the most memorable, from 1994. *Courtesy of Art Larrance.*

Above: Ray, Kurt and Rob Widmer sample a brew during the early days in their makeshift brewery. *Courtesy of Widmer Brothers Brewing.*

Left: A rare coaster from Portland's most important failed brewery, which lasted just two years. *Courtesy of Art Larrance.*

Opposite, top: Dick and Nancy Ponzi, with brewer Karl Ockert, at the grand opening of Bridgeport Brewing in 1984. *Courtesy of Karl Ockert and Bridgeport Brewing.*

Opposite, bottom: Hefeweizen is the beer that made the Widmer brothers famous and highly successful. After many years of being draft only, it was finally distributed by the bottle in 1996. *Courtesy of Widmer Brothers Brewing.*

Mike and Brian McMenamin toast the early success of their Edgefield property, circa 1993. *Courtesy of McMenamins.*

PLEASE ORDER AT THE BAR

ON TAP:	Glass	Pint	Pitcher
Falstaff	.40	.70	1.80
Heidelberg	.45	.80	2.10
Rainier	.45	.80	2.10
Schlitz Malt Liquor	.50	.95	2.60
Miller Lite	.50	.95	2.60
Miller	.50	.95	2.60
Bud	.50	.95	2.60
Henry	.50	.95	2.60
Michelob	.60	1.10	2.90
Lowenbrau L.	.60	1.10	2.90
Lowenbrau D.	.60	1.10	2.90
Ritterbrau D.	.90	1.70	4.50
Ritterbrau L.	.90	1.70	4.50
Heineken	.95	1.75	4.60
Yukon Gold	.70	1.30	3.40
Bass Ale	1.10	2.05	5.40
Whitbread	1.20	2.20	5.80
Watneys	1.10	2.00	5.30
Guinness	1.10	2.05	5.40
Grants	.95	1.80	4.70
Red Hook	.85	1.55	4.10

Also Available:
Wine, Soda Pop, Coffee, Hot Chocolate, Tea and
Dr. Zarcon's Miracle Cure

BARLEY MILL PUB

1629 S.E. Hawthorne, Portland, OR 97214 — 231-1492

This menu from the Barley Mill Pub is a nice reminder of what beer selection and prices looked like in the early 1980s. *Courtesy of McMenamins.*

Perhaps the most beloved logo in Portland craft beer belongs to Lucky Labrador Brewing, which has four locations and generally welcomes humans and their canine companions. *Photo by the author.*

This colorful Gambrinus serving tray dates to 1905. Such trays were common in saloons and restaurants of the day. *Courtesy of Bryan Anderson.*

Above: Peter Marinoff's short-lived and troubled Portland operation packaged beer in several types of bottles, as well as kegs. *Courtesy of Bryan Anderson.*

Right, top: The 1956 Blitz label celebrating one hundred years had additional color and stayed in production for several years. *Courtesy of Bryan Anderson.*

Right, bottom: Several thousand volunteers and staff make the Oregon Brewers Festival possible every year. *Courtesy of HMS Photographic and the Oregon Brewers Festival.*

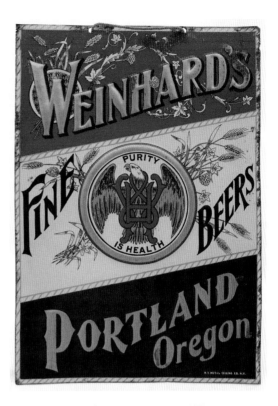

Weinhard signs like this one were likely a common sight in Portland-area saloons and stores during the 1890s. *Courtesy of Bryan Anderson.*

Lime Rickey and Sparkling Bull Run are good examples of the types of drinks that got Blitz-Weinhard through Prohibition. *Courtesy of Bryan Anderson.*

Above: Three of the most tireless ambassadors for Portland craft beer since the 1990s are (from left) Lisa Morrison, John Foyston and Chris Crabb. *Photo by author.*

Right: This serving tray depicts Henry Weinhard's most popular beer from the late nineteenth and early twentieth centuries. *Courtesy of Bryan Anderson.*

Opposite, top: This is a rare prototype of a Blitz-Weinhard promotional display from the late 1940s. This is the only known copy. *Courtesy of Bryan Anderson.*

Opposite, bottom: Rob and Kurt Widmer celebrate twenty-five years of brewing in 2009 with their favorite beers. *Courtesy of Widmer Brothers Brewing.*

Left: Portland Brewing first bottled Portland Ale in quart bottles, apparently because it was different. The first bottles were filled on December 18, 1989. *Courtesy of Art Larrance.*

Right: Saxer is one of several once promising brands that did not survive the 1990s. *Photo by the author.*

This pamphlet appeared near the end of Prohibition and attempted to address the question of wet or dry from an objective point of view. *Courtesy of Art Larrance.*

Fred Eckhardt (left) and Art Larrance kick off the 2011 Oregon Brewers Festival. Eckhardt was grand marshal of the parade, which weaves through the downtown area on the way to Waterfront Park. *Courtesy of Jay R. Brooks.*

The Horse Brass pub in Southeast Portland has been a destination for fans of imports and craft beer since the 1970s and remains so today. *Photo by the author.*

The Hedge House in Southeast Portland occupies a 1912 bungalow and is loaded with charm. It is one of five Lompoc locations. *Courtesy of Lompoc Brewing.*

My-te-fine was a Fred Meyer brand sold briefly after Prohibition, until the company's namesake pulled it from shelves. *Courtesy of Bryan Anderson.*

Brewvana Tours is one of several organizations that provide ongoing tours of the Oregon craft beer scene. *Photo by the author.*

Henry Weinhard's Blue Boar and Private Reserve Dark, successors to the original Henry's Private Reserve, did well when they appeared in the 1980s. *Courtesy of Donna McCoy. Used with permission of MillerCoors, LLC.*

Head Brewer Sean Burke adds hop pellets to a batch of Urban Farmhouse at The Commons, one of Portland's newest and fastest-growing breweries. *Photo by the author.*

After years of tapping Portland as its top market, Deschutes Brewing finally opened a brewpub in the upscale Pearl District in 2008. *Photo by the author.*

Two sides of Blitz beer. On the left is Blitz-Weinhard's first beer following Prohibition, which had less than 4 percent alcohol. On the right is near beer, sold during prohibition. *Courtesy of Bryan Anderson.*

the likeness of a local civic figure. That first year, the face on the label was the Ponzis' landlord, Roger Madden. It makes for a nice trivia question.

Food was eventually a key to success on a grand scale at Bridgeport. Early choices were rather quaint—pickled eggs, pretzels and beer nuts. There was no kitchen in the old building, so there weren't a lot of options. Finally, they came up with idea of pizza. "We tried different things," Nancy Ponzi said. "We didn't think we could make good dough efficiently at first. Then we found a way that worked. And we perfected it…a three-day process." Bridgeport pizza became legendary around town. Patrons would visit the pub for great pizza and beer. You might break your car's axel in one of the area's potholes, and you might think it was worth it. Pizza made from fresh, quality ingredients was a big draw. The Ponzis found that it wasn't particularly labor-intensive, and there was little waste because leftover ingredients were wrapped up for later use. There were few dishes to wash because they used wicker plates with paper liners. Finally, they didn't have to hire a lot of help because there was no table service. "The brewpub bill helped make us very successful," Nancy Ponzi said.

Portland Brewing was the next to open, in late March 1986. The founders were Art Larrance, Fred Bowman and Jim Goodwin, high school buddies from nearby Hillsboro. The origins of the company go back at least as far as the early 1980s, when the men were enjoying some beers one afternoon. The idea of opening a brewery came up. None of the three had any expertise in that area, but they knew Bert Grant was operating a brewery in Yakima. So they contacted Grant, who agreed to meet with them. A trip to see Grant netted a consulting agreement (they each gave him a $500 check toward the $8,500 fee) to help them start a brewery in Portland. During subsequent negotiations, Portland Brewing secured the rights to contract-brew Grant's beers for Portland. That was huge because it gave them instant credibility and a cash flow. Grant had opened the first brewpub in the country in 1982. He was selling beer beyond Yakima by 1986, and it had a good reputation and a solid following. Portland Brewing brewed nothing but Grants during its first few months as it perfected large batch versions of its own recipes.

How these three found a space for their pub and brewery is an interesting story. Searching for a space, Larrance stalked the streets of Northwest Portland. "The city told me north of Burnside, west of Broadway, east of 405," he recalled. "So I walked that area several times." Eventually, he wandered into what was then Bogart's on Northwest Fourteenth and Flanders. He told the bartender his company would soon be brewing Grant's beers in Portland and asked whether he knew of any space available

Portland Brewing Company's first brew, from January 1986. *From left to right*: Frank Commanday, Fred Bowman, Art Larrance and Bert Grant. *Courtesy of Steve Larrance.*

in the area. The bartender told him part of that building was being vacated. Thus, Portland Brewing was established in the east half of what is now the Rogue Distillery and Public House. They built a ten-barrel brewing system. Larrance and his partners are the ones who beat Dick and Nancy Ponzi to the Portland Brewing name.

Underlining the city's business-friendly climate of the time, Fred Bowman recalled an experience he had while they were preparing to open. Their pub space was small because they'd originally envisioned it as just a tasting room. Once it became a pub, they had to get a license. Bowman recalled his experience with a licensing agent during the 2010 program at the Bagdad Theater:

> *We wanted people to be able to bring in their kids so they wouldn't have to leave them on the sidewalk. An inspector came down to look the place over. I told him what we wanted to do. He said, "I just don't think I can okay it. The tables are too small, and the place just isn't going to work." I told him all I wanted is for people to be able to come in with their kids. I said, "It's too bad you don't have a rule that says, 'Underage only allowed with parent.'" He looked at me and said, "Well, we don't have that. But if you*

want to put that on the door, I'll okay the whole thing." I thought, "This is great. Here's a guy who had confidence and was willing to do something."

Portland Brewing began brewing Grant's beers for distribution by keg to local establishments on January 15, 1986. Those beers included Grant's Scottish Ale, Stout and Celtic. Portland Brewing's classic brew was Portland Ale, a light, refreshing beer. It also brewed Oregon Honey Beer, Portland Porter and Portland Stout. Several years later, after Grant had built a larger brewery in Yakima, Portland Brewing lost the Grant's franchise. It then released its own versions of Grant's beers, with minor tweaks. Grant's Scottish Ale became McTarnahan's Amber Ale, light at 3.9 percent ABV and 40 IBU. It was quite popular and eventually won a number of awards. Note the early spelling sans the "a" in "Mac," which was later changed to MacTarnahan's.

Portland Brewing began bottling in 1989, Larrance said. They went with quart bottles, as opposed to the more standard twelve-ounce bottles, because "no one else was doing quarts." The brewpub part of the Portland Brewing operation was quite successful and helped attract regular crowds. Jim Goodwin was an accomplished musician and entertained patrons, although he opted out of the business when they offered stock to the public. The company later moved out of the downtown area and relocated to the Northwest industrial area. It was subsequently rebranded as MacTarnahan's Brewing.

Of the original founding breweries, Widmer Brewing is the only one that did not immediately establish a pub, despite the fact that Kurt and Rob worked with the others to get the legislation passed. Widmer didn't have a pub until it opened the Gasthaus in 1996, long after it moved to a new location on North Russell Street. Inquiring minds may fairly wonder why. The reason is related to physical space and the success of its beer. The Lovejoy location comprised four thousand square feet of usable space. Kurt Widmer thought it was "cavernous" when he first saw it. The original plan was to use roughly half of that square footage for the brewery and the other half for a pub and offices.

Early on, the success of the beer made it apparent they would have to dedicate more space to brewing operations. "When I first looked at that space, I was sure there was plenty of room," Kurt said. "But it got away from us quickly. We badly underestimated how much space we would need for beer production." After they moved to Russell, it took them a while to get the pub up and running because they were growing too fast and had to focus on beer.

Even with the new opportunities presented by the brewpub legislation, getting the word out to prospective customers became an important issue. Media attention was crucial. Blitz-Weinhard had always received a fair amount of coverage in the *Oregonian* dating to the nineteenth century and continuing through its slow demise. Now there were multiple media outlets. Fred Eckhardt began writing a beer column for the *Oregonian* in the early '80s and continued for many years. John Foyston took over in the mid-1990s and continues to write today. *Willamette Week* joined in during the '90s and had a string of knowledgeable writers, including William Abernathy and Jeff Alworth, who informed interested readers. "The local media gave us credibility early on," Kurt Widmer recalled. "We would get a new tank, and I'd call up a few media outlets. One of the TV stations would send a camera crew and reporter, or the *Oregonian* would send someone. We got a lot of great coverage, and it helped give us credibility and get the word out."

Fred Eckhardt certainly took more than a passing interest in what was happening. As mentioned earlier, he'd been talking about the industrial swill produced by the major brands for many years. As the craft revolution ramped up, Eckhardt was in the middle of it. He not only reported on what brewers were doing but also encouraged them to try things they weren't doing. "In the early days, when there was nothing to write about, I would go around and hound the brewers to make something different," Eckhardt said. His ideas influenced brewers and beer fans in Portland and beyond. Eckhardt's 1989 book *The Essentials of Beer Style: A Catalog of Classic Beer Styles for Brewers and Beer Enthusiasts* became an indispensable guide for brewers and beer connoisseurs around the world. There can be no doubt that Portland was fortunate to have Eckhardt covering the beer beat during its formative period. Today, he carries a "Free Beer for Life" card from Widmer Brothers (Alt is reportedly his beer of choice) and is widely and deservedly considered the dean of American beer writers.

The one significant cog missing from the wheel initially was a major event to serve as a platform from which to introduce and promote a new generation of beers. The concept of a large outdoor event had occurred to Art Larrance and others prior to the time Portland Brewing, almost by accident, got involved in the blues festival that morphed into the Oregon Brewers Festival (see feature on the OBF in this chapter). The festival has played a gigantic role in the craft movement for at least two reasons. First, it was a great marketing tool because it was open to people of all ages and featured a comfortable atmosphere in which to taste craft beers; second, it has been replicated countless times on a smaller scale, thus providing ongoing

Fred Eckhardt enjoys a moment with Alan Sprints at a recent Fred Fest, a yearly event held on Eckhardt's birthday. The event honors his contributions to Portland's craft beer scene. Proceeds go to charity. *Photo by Matt Wiater, portlandbeer.org.*

opportunities to show off new beers. Two of the larger OBF spinoffs are the Holiday Ale Festival and the North American Organic Brewers Festival. There are countless smaller festivals in Portland and around the state.

There were only twenty-two beers poured at the inaugural OBF in 1988. Organizers weren't quite sure what to expect. John Harris (working for Deschutes Brewing at the time) arrived from Bend with an additional pony keg and was curtly asked, "What are you doing bringing extra beer?" Needless to say, every ounce of available beer was consumed and then some. The OBF was a big hit and has grown exponentially over the years. Larrance later bought out Bridgeport, and Widmer assumed a reduced role due to licensing issues. Today, the Oregon Brewers Festival is billed as the largest outdoor beer festival in the United States. Its values have stayed constant: an outdoor event in warm weather; tasting without judging; and families welcome. Larrance has repeatedly said he thought an outdoor beer festival modeled on Oktoberfest might be well received in Portland, but he had no idea at the outset that it would be what it is today. Held the last full weekend (soon the last full week) in July every year, the OBF is the crown jewel of Oregon Craft Beer Month and a quintessential piece of Portland's craft beer persona.

The background established by the original four breweries combined with a positive media reception and business climate to open the door through which others walked or sprinted in ensuing years. Gary Fish opened Deschutes Brewing in Bend in 1988, Jack Joyce and several partners opened what would become Rogue Brewing in Ashland in 1988 and Irene Firmat and Jerome Chicvara opened Full Sail Brewing (initially known as Hood River Brewing) in Hood River in 1987. Firmat and Chicvara apparently considered locating their operation in Portland but felt it had too many breweries and chose Hood River instead. More breweries and pubs opened in Portland, as well. Another bit of trivia: Full Sail was the first of Oregon's craft breweries to start bottling in 1987.

Essentially, the shape of Portland's modern craft beer landscape was formed during the 1980s. That doesn't mean things have stayed constant. There have been countless changes over the years. But the blueprint for success was set, and the craft movement was good to go. As it turns out, the '80s were a bridge to an even brighter future.

CHAPTER 8

BUILDING BEERVANA

CRAFT BEER GOES MAINSTREAM

It's not just because the beer is good; it's because it's ours. We know the people who make our beer…we all know each other. That makes a product taste so much better.
—*Don Younger*

With a stable foundation on which to build and shifting attitudes about what constituted good beer, Portland's craft revolution took off during the 1990s. The founding breweries expanded their operations, and newcomers soon joined in. To some extent, the movement was starting to catch on in a number of places around the country. The craft beer movement had broad roots that transcended any particular place. Portland simply turned out to be a great spot for a variety of reasons. That does not mean all was well throughout the decade, though. By the mid-'90s, there was a glut of craft beer at a time when demand flattened. As a result, there was a shakeout in which a few breweries consolidated or closed. When things finally stabilized in the early 2000s, Portland's brewery count did not immediately accelerate. In fact, the crazy growth spurt that had put the city over fifty breweries by 2013 didn't truly commence until 2009, in the midst of the worst economic downturn since the Great Depression.

Portland's original craft brewery, Bridgeport, did well throughout the '90s. The area around the brewery was just starting to experience hints of the growth that eventually transformed it, but Bridgeport maintained a rustic persona in the pub and on the nearly impassable streets outside. By all accounts, Bridgeport was a highly successful enterprise. It expanded brewing capacity and tinkered with specialty beers. The pub was busy most of the time and often packed to the gills on weekends. That may explain why the sale of Bridgeport to San Antonio–based Gambrinus (recall the nineteenth-century connection to Oregon brewing) in 1995 shocked many Portlanders. It shouldn't have. The company was doing well, and it made the Ponzis a lot of money. But Bridgeport was lagging behind Oregon competitors in both production and sales. The brewery needed upgrades and investment in marketing if it hoped to compete for market share outside the pub. The Ponzis saw the road ahead and decided to choose one of several offers in front of them and sell. It isn't a stretch to say they preferred the wine business.

Gambrinus had marketing experience. It is part of the reason Corona became popular in the United States long before it got mixed up with InBev/Anheuser-Busch. Gambrinus also had experience with a small craft brand, having bought Spoetzi Brewing of Shiner, Texas, and turned Shiner Bock into a popular brand in the state. Bridgeport represented Gambrinus' second foray into brewery ownership. It invested nearly $4 million to expand and modernize the brewery. Founding brewer Karl Ockert, who left Bridgeport in 1992 to work for Anheuser-Busch and pursue other projects, returned in 1996. He arrived just as brewers were developing an IPA recipe as part of an effort to jumpstart the company's persona. Ockert had some experience running wort through dry hops at the end of the boil. His colleagues told him that no one would drink it. But it caught on. John Foyston, who had just started writing about beer for the *Oregonian*, loved it. Bridgeport IPA won a slew of medals at the Great American Beer Festival in Denver, in part because no one was making anything quite like it. Today's IPA hop bombs have left Bridgeport IPA in the dust, but it influenced a lot of brewers in its day and helped boost the IPA style. Hop producers also took note.

As the area around the brewery transformed itself into the trendy Pearl District, it became necessary to change the pub's persona. A project to redesign the space was launched in 2004, but the upscale values were not universally appreciated when it was complete. Many preferred the pub the way it had always been. The Bridgeport folks were stuck. The trendy Pearl District demanded a different approach. High population density in the Pearl made it increasingly difficult for visitors. Thus, the upscale pub made some sense for condo dwellers and business folks. Those who were uncomfortable in the Pearl could visit Bridgeport's more rustic pub on Southeast Hawthorne, open from 1997 to 2012. The flagship location carries on with a beer lineup that relies on standards like Blue Heron Pale Ale and Bridgeport IPA, along with newer standards and rotating seasonals.

Hoping to generate new buzz, Bridgeport became the official beer sponsor of the Hillsboro Hops baseball team in 2013. The Hops are part of the Class A Northwest League and are affiliated with the Arizona Diamondbacks. A selection of Bridgeport beers, including Long Ball Ale, a beer specially made for the Hops, is available at the stadium. Another dangling piece of trivia: unbeknownst to many, Gambrinus trademarked the term "Beervana," first coined by *Willamette Week* in a 1994 guide to Portland's breweries and pubs, and uses it in Bridgeport packaging and marketing materials.

The Widmers were facing a situation similar to Bridgeport by the late 1980s. Growth had consumed the space at their Lovejoy location. More capacity was needed, and it wasn't going to happen in that location. They were approached about the possibility of setting up an upscale brewpub in a downtown location. The space was small, only two thousand square feet. But they agreed and installed a ten-barrel system with three twenty-barrel fermenters in what became known as the Heathman Bakery pub (now South Park). The added capacity bought them about a year, Kurt Widmer reckons. They were already searching for a significantly larger space, which eventually led them to tour some eighty locations around town. They couldn't afford many of the places they were interested in, particularly those in the exploding Pearl District. They finally decided on a building (actually two) on North Russell in the Lower Albina neighborhood.

At the time, Albina was a run-down, decrepit area. The structures the Widmers became interested in dated to the 1890s and had done time as storefronts, possibly a whorehouse and a flophouse for shipbuilders during World War II. Both had been empty for some time and had serious water damage, along with shattered windows. Layers of pigeon excrement covered most surfaces. Their friends told them they were crazy. It turned out the buildings were condemned and slated for demolition, which had to be approved by the city because the buildings were on the National Historic Registry. Undaunted, the Widmers submitted a plan for rehabilitation. They admittedly had no idea what they were doing. The buildings didn't cost them a penny (they paid for the property), but they spent several million dollars renovating and getting the ramshackle structures ready for business.

When the new facility opened in 1991, Widmer Brewing (as it was then known) was second to Full Sail in annual production in Oregon. The new brewery bumped production capacity to about sixty-five thousand barrels a year, barely a blip compared to what it brews today but substantial at the time. The Widmers moved quickly to capture business they had been forced to turn away earlier and soon began to think about entering the retail market with bottled beer. Full Sail had shown that bottling could be highly successful. Further motivation was provided by a former employee who helped launch Pyramid Brewing's competing Hefeweizen, which *was* bottled. As they surveyed the landscape in 1994, the Widmers expected to double their annual sales figures once they got their beer into bottles and onto store shelves. They had leased a plant in Milwaukee to brew Hefeweizen for keg distribution in the Midwest, anticipating the need to divert more of Portland's capacity to bottling. Unfortunately, things didn't work out quite the way they planned.

It soon emerged that bottling the flagship Hefeweizen presented challenges. The principle problem involved keeping the yeast in solution. Initial tests showed the yeast quickly settled once bottled. It took extensive experimentation and a proprietary process to solve the challenges related to bottling. As a result, bottled Hefeweizen was not available until 1996. Even then, early bottles included a message advising consumers to pour half the contents into a glass and swirl the remaining liquid in the bottle before adding it to the glass. Bottled Hefeweizen was a huge success (Widmer's business was up 74 percent in 1996), and they eventually bottled other brands. They also managed to get their long-awaited pub off the ground in 1996 with the opening of the Gasthaus.

Another bump in the road was related to the experience with the employee who left for Pyramid. The Widmers apparently decided to take a more serious position with respect to such competition. When brewer Alan Sprints left the company and launched Hair of the Dog Brewing in 1993, the Widmers sued him for violation of the non-compete clause in his contract. The case was eventually settled out of court to the satisfaction of neither party. "The settlement required no money," Sprints recalled. "I agreed to never brew Hefeweizen and they dropped the suit." Sprints went on to great success with Hair of the Dog (see the feature in this chapter). The Widmers incurred damage to their reputation due to the suit. In a town where people valued small artisan breweries, some saw Widmer as the big corporate guy pushing a little guy around. There was a sort of echo effect several years later as a result of their partnership with big beer. The bouts with less-than-positive PR may well have prompted them to launch programs like the Collaborator Project, which built a connection to local homebrewers and the grass-roots beer community.

The move to packaged beer cemented Widmer's dominant position in Oregon. Soon after bottling commenced, the production and bottling plant was deemed too small to meet demand. Thus, additional investment in expansion was needed. They could have taken their company public at this point; instead, the Widmers renewed efforts to find a national partner. Discussions with Miller Brewing, when the Widmers thought they were on a cusp of having bottled beer in 1994, had fizzled. By mid-1996, Anheuser-Busch had entered the fold. The St. Louis behemoth already had a Northwest partner in Seattle's Redhook, whose beers it had been rolling out across the country since 1994. But AB was diligently trying to tap into craft beer due to its rapid growth, and Widmer was an ideal partner. Both had signed off on a 1996 petition filed with the Bureau of Alcohol, Tobacco and Firearms against Jim Koch's Boston Beer Company, which was contract-brewing beers in Lake Oswego (Saxer) and Portland (Blitz-Weinhard) and marketing the beer under the name Oregon Ale and Beer Company. The BAFT complaint demanded truth in labeling and was eventually signed by thirty brewers from around the country.

Following nearly a year of rumors, speculation and no comments, Anheuser-Busch's deal to purchase a stake in Widmer was announced in April 1997. AB apparently paid just over $18 million for roughly 27 percent of Widmer common stock. People have always focused on the distribution part of the deal. Widmer, like Redhook before it, gained access to the nationwide AB distribution network as part of the deal. Just as important, the Widmers avoided the pitfalls associated with taking their company public or selling stock directly to investors. The beer geek crowd may have cried foul, but it was an ingenious business move. In effect, the Widmers maintained control of their company while deriving direct (money for expansion) and indirect (greater distribution) benefits. One of the other founding breweries chose a different path and effectively lost control of its business.

For Widmer, entering the packaged beer market was the key to signing on with AB and developing a national presence. Down the road, the deal with AB enabled Widmer to purchase Goose Island Brewing (Chicago) and form partnerships with Redhook and Kona Brewing (Hawaii). Widmer and Redhook had been contract-brewing Kona for mainland distribution (mainly a tax dodge for Kona) many years prior to forming the publicly traded Craft Brewers Alliance in 2008 (shortened to Craft Brew Alliance in 2012). The CBA bought Kona in 2010 and sold Goose Island to Anheuser-Busch in 2011 in exchange for cash, enhanced marketing support and reduced distribution fees. Although Hefeweizen is the beer that gave Widmer national recognition and made it a lot of money, sales have flattened in recent years. The brothers responded by upgrading facilities and expanding their lines of standard and specialty beers. The

CBA expanded on that theme with the launch of the gluten-free brand, Omission, in 2012, as well as Square Mile cider in 2013.

While Widmer and Bridgeport chased greater markets for their beer, the McMenamins pursued an alternative path. They were far more interested in pubs and properties than they ever were in beer. As a result, they never seriously focused on distribution of their beer beyond their own restaurants, pubs and related establishments. They had a couple dozen pubs by the early 1990s and continued to expand to the point that they had more than forty by decade's end. Names like the Bagdad Theater, Mission Theater and Crystal Ballroom instantly come to mind. Projects eventually took them out of Portland and Oregon. Two of the most momentous McMenamins projects were Edgefield in nearby Troutdale and the Kennedy School in Northeast Portland. The brothers brought both properties back to life and turned them into destinations. Their knack for resurrecting and preserving history is quite astounding, even if it sometimes makes them seem a little wacky. As the *Oregonian*'s Jonathan Nicholas so accurately reported in 1997, "Mike and Brian McMenamin are hopeless cases. Terminal. Just let them wander into an abandoned building, smell the history, soak up some memories and, boom: They're hooked."

The crown jewel in the McMenamins empire is Edgefield, a sprawling property that had the look of a monumental boondoggle when they purchased it in 1990. Built to house Multnomah County's indigent in 1911 and known then as the County Poor Farm, Edgefield served as a place for down-and-out citizens to live and work. They raised hogs, grew produce and operated a dairy, a cannery and a meatpacking plant for several decades. In 1964, the farm operation ended and the facility was renamed Edgefield Center. The main building (one of more than seventy on the property) was turned into a public nursing home known as Edgefield Manor. After the nursing home was closed in 1982, the abandoned property fell into desperate disrepair. Vagrants and vandals scribbled satanic graffiti and trashed structures. Multnomah County intended to demolish virtually everything on the property and sell the land by 1985, but the Troutdale Historical Society led a lengthy and ultimately successful battle to save it.

Mike and Brian McMenamin liked the challenge and potential presented by Edgefield. Their first order of business after they acquired the property was to find all the buildings, many of which were covered by blackberry thickets. The old cannery turned out to be a perfect place to install a twenty-barrel brewery. They also planted an organic vineyard and established Edgefield Winery that first year. To demonstrate the property's potential, they renovated the fire-damaged power station and turned it into the Power Station Pub and Theater, which opened in late 1991. Soon, they started work on turning Edgefield Manor into a lodge, which opened in 1994. Creepy old Edgefield quickly became a popular destination for folks who wanted to escape the city for a few hours or days. In some respects, Edgefield remains a work in progress even today. It features a variety of pubs and eateries, a distillery, a par-three golf and outdoor concerts in a stunning amphitheater, as well as buildings and gardens glowing with charm.

The success of the Edgefield project convinced the McMenamins a similar model might work in an urban setting. That led to their purchase of the Kennedy School in the Northeast Portland neighborhood where they grew up. Built in 1915, the school served students until it was closed in 1975 and subsequently abandoned. The place was a dilapidated hulk by the time the McMenamins got hooked on it in 1995. They paid $617,000 for the property, which they paid for by donating space to the local community for fifteen years. Although they swore not to spend more than $3.0 million on renovation, they socked more than $4.5 million into the place by the time it opened in 1997. The rejuvenated structure maintained the historic look and feel of a school (chalkboards in many rooms) while featuring a bed-and-breakfast inn, bars, pubs, a brewery, a restaurant, a theater and more. The project was mostly well-received by the Concordia neighborhood and, in fact, helped lead to a revival in the area.

The McMenamins' greatest legacy is the preservation and revitalization of historic properties like Edgefield, the Kennedy School, the Crystal Ballroom and others. They operate more than sixty establishments in Oregon and Washington as of 2013, more than half of them in the Portland area. Mike and Brian McMenamin have proven themselves to be eccentric geniuses in their choice of locations and ability to renovate and turn them into successful business ventures. Beer is most assuredly part of the legacy but certainly a secondary one. As discussed earlier, their beers (Hammerhead, Ruby, Terminator Stout and so on) were brewed mostly for their own pubs and worked well in that role. However, their great contribution to the emerging craft beer culture was their early commitment to serving good beer in multiple locations. Patrons could always choose from a tap list that included McMenamins beers, as well as those from Widmer, Portland Brewing, Bridgeport and others. They pour mostly their own beers today, but it hardly matters. The celebrated status of craft beer and McMenamins are eternally linked.

Portland Brewing was the last of the founding breweries to open and, for a variety of reasons, the first to experience financial distress. Growth had been solid through the late '80s and early '90s. Looking to capitalize on the surging demand for craft beer, the company sold stock to finance a much larger facility in industrial Northwest Portland. It moved into the new space in 1993, just as the initial wave of enthusiasm for craft beer was beginning to crest. By 1995, the market was becoming saturated, and growth started to flatten. Bridgeport solved the challenging market by selling to Gambrinus. Widmer had established itself as a dominant craft brand in the Northwest and was poised to partner with a national brand once bottling commenced. The McMenamins were diversified via their network of pubs, restaurants and related establishments. Portland Brewing, though, was in a different boat. It had a strong local identity, but really nothing more. There was no national brand waiting in the wings to partner with or buy the company.

In its effort to remain independent and viable, Portland Brewing sold common stock. This is how the founders had financed the operation from the start. The problem is they sold so much stock to a few big investors that they lost control of the company. Mac MacTarnahan, a legendary figure in Portland who had been a major investor from the start and for whom Portland Brewing's most popular beer was named, wound up owning a controlling interest. This reality didn't sit well with everyone. Cofounder Art Larrance was shown the door in late 1994. As the craft beer market was beginning to slow in 1995, Portland Brewing tried to partner with national brand Stroh, but Stroh itself was in bad shape and the deal didn't materialize. As a result of the soft market, Portland Brewing laid off 10 percent of its workforce in late 1996. MacTarnahan continued to pump money into the organization, and the company began using his name for labeling and branding in 1998. Having failed to connect with a national brand, Portland Brewing merged with Saxer Brewing of Lake Oswego in 2000. Saxer, founded in 1992, had a successful line of lagers that meshed well with the ales of Portland Brewing. Saxer brought added value by way of the Nor'Wester brands, which it acquired when Nor'Wester went broke in 1997.

The merger with Saxer was intended to create a stable regional brand worthy of a national suitor. It didn't happen. Instead, there was brand confusion, and the financial woes continued. MacTarnahan, in his mid-eighties at this point, had transferred most day-to-day business responsibilities to his son, Scott. The family was weary of sinking money into a company that seemed to be going nowhere. That conviction drove the sale to Seattle-based Pyramid in 2004. Pyramid, already strong in Washington and California, bought Portland Brewing for $4.2 million. As Scott MacTarnahan told the *Oregonian* at the time, "We couldn't keep supporting it because it just got out of hand. The only other alternative was to just to shut it down." The sale was a decent arrangement for employees, who kept their jobs, but large investors were the big winners. The three thousand or so small investors in Portland Brewing split $260,000 among them, while $3.5 million went primarily to the MacTarnahan family. Many small investors were disgruntled about receiving roughly ten cents on the dollar for their stock. But business sometimes has callous bedfellows.

Of course, the sale to Pyramid wasn't the end of Portland Brewing. Its brands lived on. Mac MacTarnahan died in March 2004, as the sale was being finalized. Pyramid was acquired by Magic Hat Brewing in 2008, and Magic Hat was itself purchased by North American Breweries in 2010. Then Costa Rica–based Florida Ice and Farm Company bought North American Brewing in 2012. Quite a wild ride. In 2013, Portland Brewing, known publicly as MacTarnahans since the late 1990s, returned to using the Portland Brewing name. The beers, sporting rebranded packaging, have been in relative free fall and are largely relegated to discount status. They are widely available in grocery and convenience stores, often at cut-rate prices, but rarely seen on draft in pubs. The rise of specialty beers has made Portland Brewing's offerings seem somewhat quaint and dated. Some of the beers are, nonetheless, quite good. Also, a number of brewers passed through Portland Brewing on their way to bigger and better things.

The momentum set in motion by the founders led to a flurry of new breweries, pubs and events through the 1990s and 2000s. With more than fifty breweries currently operating within the city, it would be impossible to discuss all of them in any detail, so we shall focus on some of the more significant and influential operations.

After he left Portland Brewing in 1994, Art Larrance continued to run the Oregon Brewers Festival. He incorporated as Cascade Brewing and opened the Raccoon Lodge in Raleigh Hills in 1998. The Raccoon Lodge has been the victim of one of Portland's more interesting truisms, which is that people from the Westside will travel to Portland's Eastside to visit pubs, but the reverse isn't generally true. Larrance remedied that situation in 2010 when he opened the Cascade Brewing Barrel House on Southeast Belmont. The Barrel House features barrel-aged sour beers, a niche that Larrance and his compatriots Ron Gansberg and Preston Weesner developed as a means of differentiating themselves from breweries engaged in what they refer to as "the hops arms race." Cascade's sour beers are produced in small batches and come at a premium price, similar to what Alan Sprints has done at Hair of the Dog. The beers have attracted local, regional and national followings. Larrance is in the process of expanding the operation via a new production facility as this book goes to press.

John Harris, a Portland brewing icon, works the kettle at Full Sail's brewery on the south waterfront. John left Full Sail after twenty years in 2012 and plans to open his own gig, Ecliptic Brewing, in late 2013. *Photo by Matt Wiater, portlandbeer.org.*

Full Sail Brewing, which had operated in Hood River since 1987, wanted a Portland presence and got it when it launched its Pilsner Room pub and brewery inside McCormick and Schmick's on the South Waterfront in 1992. John Harris, who started with McMenamins before spending several years at Deschutes Brewing in Bend, returned to Portland to assume the role of Pilsner Room brewmaster. Harris developed an early IPA there and later started the Brewmaster Reserve Program of small-batch beers. The brewery evidently supplied all the draft beer for the Portland market once it was up and running at full capacity. Harris left in 2012 to launch his own gig, Ecliptic. The Pilsner Room carries on.

Jerry Fechter arrived in Portland from Ohio in the late 1980s. He got hooked on McMenamins and Bridgeport beers while bartending and started homebrewing. Soon he wanted a brewing job, but there were no takers. Then he started working for a restaurant that wanted to brew. The result was Old Lompoc Brewing in Northwest Portland, whose first batch of beer was Erstfest in 1996. "It wasn't good," Fechter remembered. After three years, he decided to buy the place. Horse Brass owner Don Younger entered the fold as his partner, and they renamed the place New Old

The Laurelwood Brewery and Public House on Northeast Sandy Boulevard is the company's flagship location. It is supplemented by two pubs at the airport, as well as locations in Sellwood and nearby Battle Ground, Washington. *Photo by the author.*

Lompoc. They later opened the Fifth Quadrant Brewery and Pub and Sidebar tasting room on North Williams, the Hedge House on Southeast Division and the Oaks Bottom Public House on Southeast Bybee. The original brewery and pub in Northwest was demolished in 2012 but reopened as the Lompoc Tavern in 2013. The standard beers include Kick Axe Pale Ale, Proletariat Red, C-Note Imperial Pale Ale and LSD (Lompoc Special Draft). They also have a growing selection of seasonals and barrel-aged beers.

Two friends, Gary Geist and Alex Stiles, combined to create one of Portland's most memorable craft beer brands when they opened Lucky Labrador Brewing in 1994. They renovated an old roofing company building on Southeast Hawthorne and were nearly out of energy and money when they finally opened. They originally intended to call the place Lucky Dog Brewing, in honor of them being lucky to be doing something they really enjoyed. When they learned that there was a dog food by that name, they changed the name to Lucky Labrador. The Lab logo is well known and beloved around the city. While the original location on Hawthorne serves as the main brewery, the Lab has another brewery on Northwest Quimby and two satellite pubs. The beers, brewed with solar energy at the Hawthorne

ALAN SPRINTS

Alan Sprints founded Hair of the Dog Brewing in late 1993. Sprints came to Portland to study at Western Culinary Institute and later worked at Widmer for several years. But he acquired his brewing know-how mostly from the Oregon Brew Crew, an organization he led for several years. Sprints is essentially a homebrewer who started a brewery that has produced some of the most notable beers in Oregon. "I try to make beers I like, hoping others will enjoy them as well," he said.

Sprints believes in small batches and continues to use a relatively small four-barrel brewery. His approach to beer has been heavily influenced and inspired by iconic beer historian and writer Fred Eckhardt. The first Hair of the Dog beer, Adambier (later shortened to Adam), is a style that had long since ceased to exist until it was resurrected by Sprints. The idea for the beer occurred to Sprints when he heard Eckhardt speaking about beer styles that had fallen into extinction. Hair of the Dog beers have an old-world feel. You suspect that these are the sort of beers that were consumed by medieval knights. Sprints subsequently honored the contributions of Eckhardt by adding Fred to his beer list. Fred (the beer) is a high-octane ale that is deep in color, flavor and aroma.

Sprints is arguably the first brewer in town to produce barrel-aged beers, an approach that has become more or less standard with countless others. "It's nice to know my head was in the right place with barrel aging and I was ahead of the curve," he said. "Aging beers in wood is a challenge and can be good for your image."

Alan Sprints started Hair of the Dog Brewing in 1993 with the concept of producing unique, small-batch beers. He has stayed true to that goal and continues to brew his world-renowned beers on a four-barrel system. *Photo by Matt Wiater,* portlandbeer.org.

For many years, Sprints operated Hair of the Dog out of a warehouse off Holgate in Southeast Portland. It was far from the beaten path. Sprints finally decided to upgrade. The result is the brewery, tasting room and pub on Southeast Yamhill. It's where you can sample some of the best beers on the planet. A small selection of Hair of the Dog beer is available for sale in bottle-conditioned form at the pub and in stores around town. These beers, like fine wine, are generally thought to improve with age. But they also taste great right out of the tap.

pub since 2007, have always been drinkable and have improved in recent years. The aptly named Super Dog IPA is a local favorite.

Laurelwood's first pub opened in 2001, taking over a space in Northeast Portland's Hollywood District previously occupied by the recently defunct Old World Pub and Brewery. Owner Mike DeKalb had a strong restaurant background but didn't know much about beer. So, he made a wise move and hired former Old World and onetime Bridgeport brewer Christian Ettinger as his first brewer. Ettinger was a pioneer (along with Craig Nichols of Alameda Brewing, who went on to found the now defunct Roots Brewing and the North American Organic Beer Festival) of organically brewed beers. Laurelwood quickly became a popular destination for neighborhood families and seekers of great beer. It outgrew its space long before moving to a much larger one on Sandy Boulevard in 2007.

Ettinger left Laurelwood to found Hopworks Urban Brewery soon thereafter. His former assistant, Chad Kennedy, replaced him and carried on. When Kennedy left in 2011 to help put together Worthy Brewing in Bend, Vasili Gletsos replaced him and has taken the brewing operation to new levels of creativity. Today, Laurelwood has several Portland locations, including two at the airport and a recently opened pub in Sellwood. It also operates a small brewery and pub in Battle Ground, Washington, twenty miles north of Portland. In June 2013, Laurelwood announced that some of its most popular beers will be contract-brewed by the Craft Brew Alliance for bottle distribution, allowing it to focus more on specialty beers in its pubs. The beat goes on.

When Gary Fish founded Deschutes Brewing in 1988, he chose Bend because he and his family liked central Oregon. Deschutes was an immediate success and grew quickly. The company finally opened a brewery and pub in Portland in 2008. It's fair to wonder what took so long. "We wanted to get to Portland for many years, but we always seemed to be dealing with growth issues in Bend," Fish said. "Portland was always our top market, and the first place we pursued a real sales strategy. So I feel like we've always been there." Deschutes opened its upscale pub in the Pearl District just as the Great Recession of 2008 was kicking in. They were welcomed with open arms. Today, Deschutes is the fifth-largest craft brewer in the country, with a solid regional and national presence. Fish announced an employee stock ownership plan in 2013. Did he see any of it coming in the beginning? "No sane person would have," he said.

Like Deschutes, Rogue Brewing doesn't figure prominently in the early history of craft beer in Portland. Jack Joyce and several partners founded Rogue in Ashland in 1988. They soon moved to a larger space in Newport. John Maier, a former aircraft technician, was hired as brewmaster and created solid beers that attained a good following in Oregon and beyond. Rogue Public House and (later) Distillery opened in Portland late 2000 on Northwest Flanders in the space once occupied by Portland Brewing and Bogart's. The pub was an instant success.

A few years later, in 2008, Rogue bought the Green Dragon in Southeast Portland. The Green Dragon, named after the Boston pub from whence Paul Revere launched his infamous midnight ride, had a reputation for serving great beer but also had financial problems. Many beer fans feared Rogue would turn the place upside down and ruin it. Instead, Rogue installed an additional thirty taps and expanded the beer selection. The Buckman Botanical Brewery, Rogue's small experimental brewery, operates inside the Green Dragon and creates a plethora of interesting beers. Joyce and company added another Portland location when they opened a pub near Portland State University in 2011. Rogue also has a pub at the airport. Although it wasn't here at the start, its beers and pubs have a solid reputation in Portland.

In addition to the founding breweries and the significant second wavers, there have been a number of important recent launches. Places like The Commons, Upright and Breakside Brewing have explored Belgian influences and barrel aging to create unique brews. Some of the other names to remember include Alameda, Amnesia, Base Camp, Burnside, Coalition, Columbia River, Gigantic, Harvester (gluten-free beers), Migration, Occidental, Pints and Sasquatch. Of course, you don't have to brew to serve great beer. Portland has a growing number of taprooms and pubs (some that were formerly dive taverns) that are serving up fantastic beers in the vein of the Horse Brass. Places like Apex, Bailey's, Beermongers, Belmont

Velo Cult, located in the Hollywood District, is a recent addition and leans on the popularity of beer and cycling. A great tap list, friendly atmosphere and unique events add to the fun. *Photo by the author.*

Station, Blitz (several locations), Bottles, Bridgetown Beerhouse, Concordia Ale House, Hawthorne Hophouse (two locations), the Hop & Vine, the Moon and Sixpence, Oregon Public House, Roscoe's and Saraveza have become destinations for hardcore beer fans. Brew supply stores like F.H. Steinbart, Let's Brew, Portland U-Brew and Pub and Uptown Market promote good beer by providing education, supplies and brewing facilities. Many movie theaters have joined the craft beer buzz as well, borrowing from McMenamins. Taking a step in another direction is Velo Cult, which opened in 2012, a combination bike shop and pub, with great beer and a calendar filled with events. Creative approaches to marketing craft beer alongside other popular themes and activities in Portland seem nearly endless and are evolving virtually by the minute.

Related to the marketing conversation is the recent trend toward increasingly hoppy beers. India Pale Ale, popular in Portland and Oregon for many years, is now the most popular craft beer style in the country. Oregon IPAs tend to rely more on hop flavor and aroma than bitterness. There's a reason for that. Oregon's Willamette Valley (south of Portland) led the nation in hops production until 1950. Then the Yakima area in

Washington State became the top dog and has been ever since, its primary customers being big beer. Looking for ways to stay relevant, Willamette Valley growers and Oregon State University developed new hop varieties that feature aroma and flavor. This trend has accelerated in recent years. The proximity to designer hops has enabled Oregon brewers to lead the way in the production of styles that rely heavily on hop aroma and flavor. IPA is the most popular, but it is not the only example. These beers do not travel well in bottles or kegs. They must be experienced fresh in Oregon to be fully appreciated—one of the reasons Portland has become a prime destination.

At the end of the day, you cannot overlook the contributions from those who have informed and promoted craft beer in a variety of ways. The benchmark established by Fred Eckhardt was carried forward by John Foyston, William Abernathy, Jeff Alworth, Lisa Morrison and others. The many beer blogs that cover Portland's beer scene today are merely descendants of the informed efforts of days and years gone by. There is no denying the Oregon Brewers Festival's role in setting the stage for other promotional events large and small, including the Portland International Beer Festival, the Holiday Ale Festival and the North American Organic Beer Festival, among others. No one has contributed more promotional value over the years than Chris Crabb, Art Larrance and Don Younger. The late Carl Simpson belongs in that group, as well. Jim and Bobby Kennedy, who operated Admiralty Distributing in the early days, helped build credibility for craft beer when mainstream distributors weren't going to bother. Finally, today's rabid beer scene has escalated to the point that tours have become a great way to see and learn a lot quickly. Brewvana Tours, founded in 2011, is one of several entities that provide that service.

WHY PORTLAND?

Portland was once known as the scariest port, which contributes to the appeal and storyline. All the elements were just right here. You can shake up a cocktail and it won't be right unless everything balances out.

—Lisa Morrison

The preceding pages delved into the development of beer and brewing in Portland. Today, the city is home to one of the most vibrant beer cultures in the world—maybe *the* most vibrant. There are more than fifty operating breweries in the city, with more on the way. The line between styles is blurring with each passing week, month and year. There are numerous pubs, restaurants, theaters and related enterprises that lean on good beer to attract customers. The beer event calendar is stacked to the hilt, and not just during the busy summer season. You'll find some sort of craft beer–related event happening virtually every day in Portland. A lot of people are making a good living in the business of craft beer. Distributors, who were initially concerned that brewpubs might hurt their business, are making big money on craft beer. The industry funnels millions of dollars into Portland's economy each year and shows really no signs of slowing down. Success like that demands an explanation. Why Portland? How did a small city on the West Coast become Beervana? It's a relevant question.

Despite the significant contributions of breweries that have opened in the last decade or so, the foundation for what exists today was built in the 1980s by the founding breweries. It's clear enough who they are. They successfully navigated challenges that paved the way for what came later. Many have suggested explanations for their success: it was the water; it was the proximity to quality ingredients; and it was the strong pub culture dating to the nineteenth century, encouraged by foul weather that forces residents inside for much of the year. These are all fine explanations and likely played a role in what occurred here. But they seem simplistic. In fact, many American cities have access to good water and ingredients. Lots of places have dreadful weather that forces citizens to seek refuge in pubs. Portland has all of these things, for sure, but it is not alone.

The first things that weigh heavily are the very strong sense of provincialism and independence in Portland. The relatively small size of the city may account for these influences, which date to the nineteenth century. Provincialism encouraged a strong do-it-yourself culture and an acceptance of things that were local, handmade and different. Brewers could go to pubs where patrons, who were quite satisfied with whatever macro beer they were drinking, would give craft beer a try. It caught on. Collaboration and cooperation have also been common themes. There was always an element of competitiveness, but early brewers didn't function as competitors. Instead, they worked together to refine their craft and pass the crucial brewpub legislation. Just as important, because three of the founding breweries were located near each other in Northwest Portland, they were able to share orders for hops and grains at a time when suppliers were not accustomed to selling in small increments. That became less important as they grew, but it was significant at the start.

The shadow of Blitz-Weinhard also looms large in this conversation. It was the lofty stature of the old brewery that provided Portland with a strong link to local beer. The 1976 release of Henry Weinhard's Private Reserve, a premium product that targeted discriminating beer drinkers, effectively predicted the coming of craft beer a decade later. Blitz-Weinhard might well have been part of that revolution had it been smaller. Obviously, other cities had influential breweries dating to the nineteenth century. But Weinhard was a large brewery situated in a small city that grew up around it, which magnified its influence on consumers, brewers and entrepreneurs. The city's strong preference for draft beer (17 percent of beer consumed is draft versus 10 percent in most cities) may also be traced at least partially to Weinhard. Finally, Blitz-Weinhard brewers assisted the early craft brewers in a variety of ways, often secretly, which helped them improve quality. Even as the old brewery staggered toward the end in the 1990s, it was held in high esteem by the community. That is significant.

Another often overlooked factor in the rise of Oregon craft beer is tax policy. It should not be ignored. Oregon breweries have benefited from a historically low per-barrel excise tax of roughly $2.60, a little more than 8 cents per gallon. "You can't overstate the importance of tax laws," said Kurt Widmer. "We have the fourth-lowest beer excise tax in the country, and the state has chosen not to tax us out of business. Many people outside the business don't appreciate the importance of that." Whenever the state legislature suggests the idea of raising the beer tax, the industry springs into action and prevents it. This has been a boon to breweries throughout Oregon, although Portland's breweries benefited by being in the state's largest city and by being first. Along these lines, Portland's early entry into craft beer provided a large pool of enthusiastic and opportunistic brewers, many of whom later went on to start their own breweries. Some of the city's most prominent names today got their start at Widmer, Portland Brewing, Bridgeport or McMenamins. A graphic documenting this reality appeared in the July 2013 issue of *Portland Monthly* magazine.

While considering the exploits of craft beer in Portland, it's significant to note that the movement did not start here. Washington and California had brewpubs and craft breweries before Portland did. It may be reasonably argued that the roots of the greater movement that eventually launched craft beer originated in California and were subsequently adopted by Seattle and Portland. That's certainly a viable argument in terms of the West Coast. The greater movement itself was underway by the 1960s and represented a paradigm shift away from the lighter preferences of the prior generation. Instead of industrially processed, prepackaged, often flavorless foods and drinks, a growing number of Americans came to prefer things that were full of flavor, local and handmade.

It might seem a wacky leap, but shifting tastes were suggested by Julia Child's legendary 1961 book *Mastering the Art of French Cooking*. Child's ideas about cooking and food may not be directly relevant to beer, but the idea of richer, fuller, more flavorful food prepared in an artisan fashion had a universal effect on the mindset of Americans, as well as on their interest in trying things that were new and better. The exploding interest in homebrewing definitely evolved from that mindset. The movement itself was not monolithic or universal. Some parts of the country, particularly much of the old Confederacy, were slow to join or never did join the movement. At the same time, there were parts of the country where the notions were embraced right away. On the West Coast, the San Francisco Bay Area, Portland and Seattle were hotspots.

A strong argument can be made that the Bay Area was the center of this movement. Several idealistic partners founded the iconic Chez Panisse in Berkeley in 1971. Its objective was to feature locally sourced ingredients prepared by artisan chefs. The Chez Panisse concept eventually spread to Seattle and Portland. Better coffee was also part of this movement, and here again, the Bay Area figures in the conversation. The three partners who formed Starbucks in Seattle in 1971 met while studying at the University of San Francisco. Their original idea was to sell high-quality coffee beans and equipment to the public. It's a forgotten detail, but Starbucks did not brew coffee in the early days; that came later. Chez Panisse and Starbucks are merely examples of an emerging shift in tastes that started small and were based on the concept of higher-quality food and drink. Anchor and New Albion Brewing, both located in the Bay Area, suggested the future of beer.

There were other big picture factors that played into the emerging movement. The baby boom generation, battered by the turbulent 1960s, became focused on health and the environment during the 1970s. Portland embraced that thinking early on. How could ideas like that possibly wind up serving as a basis for the coming revolution in beer? Part of the answer lies in the reaction to chemically enhanced, preprocessed foods and drinks. People became worried about toxins contaminating what they were eating and drinking. A sort of health-conscious snobbery emerged. If you were going to eat or drink something not nominally considered healthy, why not move away from cheap junk and go with high quality items? That mindset helped advance the food, coffee and craft beer revolutions. If you were going to drink a beer, why not limit yourself to one and make it something good? The growing popularity of imports and homebrewed beers during the 1970s reflected that altered mindset. Craft beer fit with it perfectly when it arrived. Portland embraced these shifts in thinking and taste.

Nancy Ponzi offered a nice explanation of shifting tastes and how they relate to beer in a 2013 interview:

> *The transformation of food that happened here and has spread across the country was huge. We had nothing in the '60s as far as culinary. Then you saw the beginning of the environmental movement and the search for better food, better coffee, better wine, local and organic, etc. We'd go to Europe and see all these little markets. Now we have those everywhere here. It's transformed. There were several things that came together as part of the transformation, and beer was a part of that.*

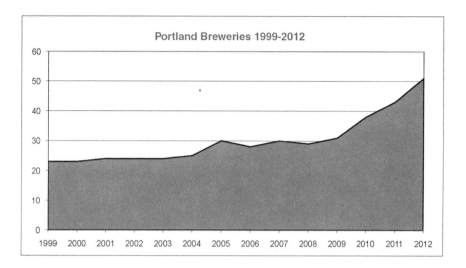

This graph suggests 40 percent of Portland brewery growth has happened since 2009. *Based on data provided by the Oregon Brewers Guild.*

When you look at Portland's current landscape of brewpubs, coffee shops, great restaurants, farmers' markets, wineries, organic grocery stores and community gardens, all of these things flowed from a movement that was born in the 1960s and grew slowly through the late 1970s. It then got a foothold and continued to reinvent itself over the course of ensuing decades. Portland was most certainly not the center of that movement, but the citizens of Portlandia embraced it. In beer terms, the conditions helped facilitate a revolution that has flourished to this day. As Lisa Morrison said, things balanced out perfectly for Portland and beer. This is perhaps why the city is widely regarded as the beer capital of the world.

The future seems quite bright, but no one knows where it leads. The recent fixation on IPAs and heavily hopped beers appears to be moderating. Wacky blends are the new rage, and established styles and brands are seemingly in decline. Will barrel-aged beers gain a stronger foothold? Will the event barrage continue? One of the more momentous questions involves the twenty-plus breweries that have opened since 2009. They represent roughly 40 percent of the city's total. The trend isn't limited to Portland, as it's happened in other places, too. But we're talking about a lot of breweries in a city that was shaken by the financial meltdown of 2008–9. The economy still hasn't fully recovered, yet you have all these breweries opening, beginning in 2009. Changing demographics via a continued influx of twenty-one- to thirty-five-year-olds who "come here to retire" may offer a partial explanation, but there must be more. There are those who worry that a craft beer bubble is forming—that it may burst one day. It's difficult to say. On its present course, Portland will inevitably reach the point when it produces more beer than it can consume or export. There's also the possibility of another paradigm shift in tastes. The American past is littered with such shifts. Alas, these are contemporary issues for someone else to grapple with down the road.

SB 813 (BREWPUB BILL)

R elating to alcoholic liquor; creating new provisions; amending ORS 471.290; and declaring an emergency. Be it Enacted by the People of the State of Oregon:

Section 1. A bed and breakfast license may be issued to the owner or operator of a private residence that is not a boarding house but that accommodates transients for a limited duration and shall allow the sale or service by the licensee or any employee of malt beverages containing not more than eight percent of alcohol by weight, and wine containing not more than 21 percent of alcohol by volume to guests for consumption on the licensed premises only. The license does not permit sale or service to or consumption by the general public or employees of the premises.

Section 2. ORS 471.290 is amended to read: 471.290.

(1) Any person desiring a license or renewal of a license shall make application to the commission upon forms to be furnished by the commission showing the name and address of the applicant, the applicant's citizenship, location of the place of business which is to be operated under the license, and such other pertinent information as the commission may require. No license shall be granted or renewed until the provisions of the Liquor Control Act and the rules of the commission have been complied with. (2) Except as provided in this section, the commission shall assess a nonrefundable fee for processing

each application for any license authorized by ORS chapter 471 or 472, in an amount equal to 25 percent of the annual license fee. The commission shall not begin to process any license application until the application fee is paid. If the commission allows an applicant to apply at the same time for alternative licenses at one premises, only the application fee for the most expensive license shall be required. If a license is granted or committed, the application fee of 25 percent shall be applied against the annual license fee. This subsection shall not apply to an agent's license, a salesman's license, a manufacturer certificate of approval, a druggist's license, a health care facility license or to any license which is issued for a period of less than 30 days.

(3) Subject to subsection (4) of this section, the commission shall assess a nonrefundable fee for processing a renewal application for any license authorized by ORS chapter 471 or 472 only if the renewal application is received by the commission less than 20 days before expiration of the license. If the renewal application is received prior to expiration of the license but less than 20 days prior to expiration, this fee shall be 25 percent of the annual license fee. If a renewal application is received by the commission after expiration of the license but no more than 30 days after expiration, this fee shall be 40 percent of the annual license fee. This subsection shall not apply to an agent's license, a salesman's license, a manufacturer certificate of approval, a druggist's license, a health care facility license, a brewery-public house license or to any license which is issued for a period of less than 30 days.

(4) The commission may waive the fee imposed under subsection (3) of this section if it finds that failure to submit a timely application was due to unforeseen circumstances or to a delay in processing the application by the local governing authority that is no fault of the licensee.

(5) The annual license fee is nonrefundable and shall be paid by each applicant upon the granting or committing of a license. The annual license fee and the minimum bond required of each class of license are as follows:

SECTION 3. Licensing details and fees [omitted]

SECTION 4. (1) A brewery-public house license shall allow the licensee:

(a) To manufacture annually on the licensed premises, store, transport, sell to wholesale malt beverage and wine licensees of the commission and export no more than 10,000 barrels of malt beverages containing not more than eight percent of alcohol by weight;

(b) To sell malt beverages manufactured on or off the licensed premises at retail for consumption on the premises;

(c) To sell malt beverages in brewery-sealed packages at retail directly to the consumer for consumption off the premises;

(d) To sell on the licensed premises at retail malt beverages manufactured on the licensed premises in unpasteurized form directly to the consumer for consumption off the premises, delivery of which may be made in a container supplied by the consumer; and

(e) To conduct the activities described in paragraphs (b) to (d) of this subsection at one location other than the premises where the manufacturing occurs.

(2) A brewery-public house licensee, or any person having an interest in the licensee, is not eligible for a brewery license authorized by ORS 471.220 or a wholesale malt beverage and wine license authorized by ORS 471.235.

(3) A brewery-public house licensee, or any person having an interest in the licensee, may also hold a winery license authorized by ORS 471.223.

(4) A brewery-public house licensee is eligible for a retail malt beverage license and for special one-day retail beer licenses. All sales and delivery of malt beverage to the retail malt beverage licensed premises must be made only through a wholesale malt beverage and wine licensee.

(5) For purposes of ORS chapter 473, a brewery public house licensee shall be considered to be a manufacturer.

SECTION 5. This Act being necessary for the immediate preservation of the public peace, health and safety, an emergency is declared to exist, and this Act takes effect on its passage.

Approved by the Governor July 13, 1985
Filed in the office of Secretary of State July 15, 1985

BEEROLOGY

ale: Beer made with top fermenting yeast. Ale yeast ferments at higher temperatures and produces beers with a different character than lagers (the other beer).

ale house: A place that serves beer in draft and/or bottled form but has no brewery on-site. This place may also be known as a tap house or pub.

barley wine: Strong ale, typically between 8 and 14 percent ABV. Barley wines are popular winter beers and tend to age well.

barrel: For beer purposes, a barrel is thirty-one gallons.

Beermuda Triangle: A loosely defined and expanding area of southeast Portland where the number of breweries and pubs is nearly impossible to count.

bottle fermentation: A process by which beer is wholly or partially fermented in a bottle (could also be a cask) by adding a small amount of unfermented wort or sugar and sometimes yeast prior to capping. The objective of bottle conditioning is normally to carbonate the beer; however, it may be used to achieve enhanced flavors, particularly in high-gravity beers that are likely to be aged for several years.

brewpub: A brewpub is a pub or restaurant that sells beer produced on the premises. Breweries that don't have a partner pub or restaurant often have a tasting room.

cask-conditioned: Beer that is unfiltered, unpasteurized and carbonated during secondary fermentation inside a cask. Cask-conditioned beers are served from the cask without injecting additional gas. They are usually served warmer with less carbonation than beer served from a standard keg. Fans of cask beer often point to enhanced flavors.

craft brewery: The Colorado-based Brewers Association defines a craft brewery as "small, independent and traditional" and gives a production size of less than 6 million U.S. beer barrels. Of all the breweries in the United States, fewer than one hundred are *not* considered craft brewers.

dry-hopped: The practice of adding hops (usually in pellet form) to beer that has completed primary fermentation. Dry hopping adds flavor and aroma, typically without adding bitterness.

fermentation: Occurs when yeast converts the sugars in wort to alcohol, CO_2 and other components.

fresh-hopped beer: Beers that are made around hop harvest time in the late summer and early fall when brewers use fresh hops, as opposed to those that have been dried, to brew. Fresh-hopped beers have gained a following in recent years.

growler: A glass jug typically available in thirty-two- and sixty-four-ounce sizes. Some modern versions are insulated to keep beer cold. Breweries and pubs sell and refill growlers with draft beer for consumption elsewhere. The term is passed down from the nineteenth century, when growlers were metal pails with covers that vibrated or "growled" when carried.

IBU: International Bittering Units. This number provides a general idea of how bitter a beer will be. High IBUs (above 50) in a darker beer are often hidden by malty flavors. Low IBUs can sometimes be overwhelming in a light beer. A typical IPA will probably have an IBU value of 60 or more.

IPA: India Pale Ale. Originally made to quench the thirst of British colonial soldiers in India, IPA had higher alcohol content and more hops to preserve it in transit. IPA has been adopted as the preferred beer style in the Northwest and became the top craft beer style nationwide in 2011.

lager: Beer made with bottom fermenting yeast that functions in cool or cold environs. The prevailing assumption among some novice beer fans is that lager beers are defined as Bud, Coors, Miller and so on. In fact, many complex beers, including dark ones, are lagers.

nitro: Nitrogen is sometimes used in place of CO_2 when dispensing certain beers because it helps form a rich head and contributes to a smooth feel in the mouth.

rotating tap: Many pubs, eateries and some brewpubs have taps that are not reserved for specific beers; instead, a variety of beers rotate through. These are less common in brewpubs because they prefer to sell their own beer. Portland's best pubs and tap houses have between ten and fifty rotating taps.

session beer: Typically, a low-alcohol beer that can be consumed in significant quantity over a period of hours without causing incoherence or stupor.

sour beer: A beer style characterized by tart or sour taste. Sour beer has gained popularity in recent times but remains largely a niche style. In practice, any beer may be soured, intentionally or unintentionally. Souring may be achieved through yeast strains or bacteria. The most common agent used is lactobacillus, an anaerobic bacteria.

taster tray: A plate or tray of beers in small glasses, typically between two and four ounces. It might also be called a sampler tray or beer flight.

BIBLIOGRAPHY

BOOKS

Alworth, Jeff. *The Best of Beervana*. Portland, OR: Walking Man Press, 2011.

Burgess, Robert J. *Silver Bullets: A Soldier's Story of How Coors Bombed in the Beer Wars*. New York: St. Martin's Press, 1993.

Crouch, Andy. *Great American Craft Beer: A Guide to the Nation's Finest Beers and Breweries*. Philadelphia, PA: Running Press Book Publishers, 2010.

Eckhardt, Fred. *The Essentials of Beer Style: A Catalog of Classic Beer Styles for Brewers and Beer Enthusiasts*. Portland, OR: Eckhardt Associates, 1989.

Gaston, Joseph. *Portland, Oregon: Its History and Builders*. Vol. 2. Portland, OR: S.J. Clarke Publishing Company, 1911.

Heying, Charles. *Brew to Bikes: Portland's Artisan Economy*. Portland, OR: Ooligan Press, 2010.

Holbrook, Stewart H. *Holy Old Mackinaw: A Natural History of the American Lumberjack*. New York: MacMillan Company, 1957.

John, Finn J.D. *Wicked Portland: The Wild and Lusty Underworld of a Frontier Seaport Town*. Charleston, SC: The History Press, 2012.

MacColl, E. Kimbark. *The Growth of a City: Power and Politics in Portland, Oregon 1915 to 1950*. Portland, OR: Georgian Press, 1979.

———. *The Shaping of a City: Business and Politics in Portland, Oregon 1885 to 1915*. Portland, OR: Georgian Press, 1976.

MacColl, E. Kimbark, with Harry H. Stein. *Merchants, Money & Power: The Portland Establishment 1843–1913*. Portland, OR: Georgian Press, 1988.

Meier, Gary, and Gloria Meier. *Brewed in the Pacific Northwest: A History of Beer Making in Oregon and Washington*. Seattle, WA: Fjord Press, 1991.

Morrison, Lisa M. *Craft Beers of the Pacific Northwest: A Beer Lover's Guide to Oregon, Washington and British Columbia*. Portland, OR: Timber Press, 2011.

Ogle, Maureen. *Ambitious Brew: The Story of American Beer*. New York: Harcourt Inc., 2008.

Okrent, Daniel. *Last Call: The Rise and Fall of Prohibition*. New York: Simon & Schuster, 2010.

Papazian, Charlie. *The New Complete Joy of Homebrewing*. New York: Harper Paperbacks, 2003.

Pintarich, Paul. *History by the Glass...a Second Round: Portland's Past and Present Saloons, Bars and Taverns*. Portland, OR: Bianco Publishing, 2007.

Ronnenberg, Herman. *Beer and Brewing in the Inland Northwest, 1850–1950*. Moscow: University of Idaho Press, 1993.

Smith, Gregg. *Beer in America: The Early Years—1587–1840*. Boulder, CO: Sirus Books, 1998.

Snyder, Eugene E. *Skidmore's Portland: His Fountain and Its Sculptor*. Portland, OR: Binford & Mort, 1973.

Tremblay, Victor J., and Carol H. Tremblay. *The US Brewing Industry: Data and Economic Analysis*. Cambridge, MA: MIT Press, 2005.

Van Munching, Philip. *Beer Blast: The Inside Story of the Brewing Industry's Bizarre Battles for Your Money*. New York: Random House, 1997.

GOVERNMENT DOCUMENTS

Oregon legislature. *Laws and Resolutions Enacted and Adopted by the Sixty-Second Legislative Assembly at its Special Session on July 30, 1984, and by the Sixty Third Legislative Assembly at Its Regular Session Beginning January 13 and Ending June 21, 1985*. Vol. 2. Salem, OR: State Printing Office, 1,313–15.

———. *Legislative Minutes Relating to SB 813*. May 14–June 17, 1985. Printed transcript available though Oregon State Archives.

ARTICLES

A special note with regard to the Oregonian: *I used the Multnomah County Library's online research tool to source several hundred articles from the* Oregonian, *Portland's longest-running and most significant newspaper. The reporting dedicated to beer and related topics is extensive from the 1890s on—history's first draft, if you will. For reasons of space, the specific articles used are not cited or listed here. Electronic versions of all articles are in my possession.*

Buckingham, Lucy. "Mapping Beervana." *Portland Monthly* (July 2013): 56–57.

Carroll, Glenn, and Anand Swaminathan. "Why the Microbrewery Movement? Organizational Dynamics of Resource Partitioning in the U.S. Brewing Industry." *American Journal of Sociology* 106, no. 3 (2000): 715–62.

Caswell, John E. "The Prohibition Movement in Oregon II: 1904–1915." *Oregon Historical Quarterly* 40, no. 1 (March 1939): 64–92.

Cizmar, Martin. "Beer of the Future: A New Era of Oregon Hops Will Better Your Brew." *Willamette Week* (February 15, 2012).

Donnelly, Robert C. "Organizing Portland: Organized Crime, Municipal Corruption and the Teamsters Union." *Oregon Historical Quarterly* 104, no. 3 (Fall 2003): 334–65.

Jones, Andrew. "Craft Brewing Defines Oregon as U.S. 'Beer Capital.'" *National Geographic News* (August 10, 2001).

Libby, Brian. "Beer Legend Don Younger." *Imbibe* (July/August 2006).

Mills, Joshua. G. "Heileman Brewing to Be Sold for $390 Million." *New York Times*, November 2, 1993.

Piece, Jason. "The Winds of Change: The Decline of Extractive Industries and the Rise of Tourism in Hood River County, Oregon." *Oregon Historical Quarterly* 108, no. 3 (Fall 2007): 410–31.

Woodward, Bob, and Laurel Bennett. "Oregon Beer History: The Brave History of Brewing's Triumph Over Time." *1859 Magazine* (Summer 2009).

ELECTRONIC MEDIA

Oregon Historical Society and McMenamins. "History Pub at the Bagdad Theater." Presented on August 30, 2010. Unpublished DVD in possession of Art Larrance and McMenamins.

Oregon Public Broadcasting. *Beervana* (Oregon Experience Documentary). Beth Harringon, producer/writer, 2007. Viewable online at www.opb.org.

INTERVIEWS

Many interviews were conducted in person and recorded. The recordings and transcripts of those and other interviews, as well as email correspondence, are in possession of the author.

Alworth, Jeff. Personal interview, January 31, 2013.

Anderson, Bryan. Personal interview, November 27, 2012.

Bowman, Fred. Phone interview, March 25, 2013.

Crabb, Chris. Personal interview, February 28, 2013.

Fechter, Jerry. Personal interview, March 6, 2013.

Fish, Gary. E-mail correspondence, March 27, 2013.

Foyston, John. Personal interview, March 6, 2013.

Harris, John. Personal interview, February 18, 2013.

Larrance, Art. Personal interview, June 29, 2011; November 27, 2012; May 15, 2013.

Mason, Tom. Phone interview, February 26, 2013.

McMenamin, Brian. Personal interview, January 10, 2013.

Morrison, Lisa. Personal interview, April 9, 2013.

Ockert, Karl. Personal interview, February 14, 2013.

Ponzi, Dick and Nancy. Personal interview, March 15, 2013.

Romaine, Paul. Phone interview, February 12, 2013.

Sprints, Alan. E-mail correspondence, April 12, 2013.

Widmer, Kurt. Phone interview, May 13, 2013.

Widmer, Kurt and Rob. Personal interview, November 27, 2012.

UNPUBLISHED MATERIALS

Ingraham, Aukjen Tadema. "Henry Weinhard: Portland's Elusive Founding Father." Senior thesis, Whitman College, Walla Walla, Washington, 1998.

Turnblom, Kevin W. "Oregon Beer: The Fall and Rise of Craft Brewing." Department of History Senior thesis, Weber State University, Ogden, Utah, December 2006.

INDEX

ABOUT THE AUTHOR

Pete Dunlop has been enjoying Oregon craft beers since 1989. Before arriving in Portland, he earned a master's degree in history at Washington State University. Since coming to the Portland area, Pete has taught high school journalism and worked in marketing communications for several organizations. Although he has not worked in the craft beer industry, he has followed it closely and has many years of experience as a homebrewer and blogger. Cheers to you for buying and reading this book. Visit the companion blog at beervanabuzz.com.